# al fresco
## COOKING

# al fresco
## COOKING

CAROLYN HUMPHRIES

**foulsham**
LONDON • NEW YORK • TORONTO • SYDNEY

# foulsham

The Publishing House, Bennetts Close,
Cippenham, Slough, Berkshire, SL1 5AP, England

ISBN 0-572-03082-7

Copyright © 2005 W. Foulsham & Co. Ltd

A CIP record for this book is available from the British Library

Previously published as *Summer Weekend Cookbook*

Photographs by Carol and Terry Pastor
Cover photograph © Anthony Blake Picture Library
Text illustrations by Sophie Azimont

Scalloped plate (shown on page 78) courtesy of Isis Ceramics, The Old Toffee Factory, Oxford.
Bowl and spoon (shown on page 103) courtesy of Ingredients, Castle Mall, Norwich.

Printed in Great Britain by St Edmundsbury Press Ltd, Bury St Edmunds, Suffolk.

# Contents

# Introduction

Eating out of doors on a hot, sunny day or a warm, balmy evening is one of life's greatest pleasures. Even a humble sandwich can taste fantastic in the open air. But anyone can knock up a filling between two slices of bread. This book is about real eating: food for every possible outdoor meal. From barbecues to garden parties, stylish picnics to family get-togethers and even clever ideas for what to eat when you stagger home from work, hot, tired and hungry. There are lots of tips on getting it right too, from advance planning and what to drink to what you'll need in the way of crockery, cutlery or other equipment for the feast you have in mind.

## NOTES ON THE RECIPES

- Ingredients are given in metric, imperial and American measures. Use only one set in a recipe; do not try and combine them.

- Always wash, dry, peel and core, when necessary, fresh ingredients before use.

- Preparation and cooking times are approximate and should be used as a guide only.

- All herbs called for are fresh unless otherwise stated. If substituting dried, use half the amount or less as they are very pungent.

- All spoon measures are level:
  1 tsp = 5 ml
  1 tbsp = 15 ml

- Hens' eggs are medium unless otherwise stated in the recipe.

- A few recipes use raw eggs; do not give to young children or invalids.

- Aways preheat the oven and cook on the shelf just above the centre unless otherwise stated. (This does not apply to fan-assisted models.)

- ❄ means the recipe can be frozen.

# Weekend Picnics

Packing up for a day in the hills with friends or at the sea *en famille* with seriously good food needs a bit of planning. But if you prefer to be more spontaneous (and with the British climate, it tends to have to be that way), then cook in advance so you'll have some delicious little numbers stored in the freezer. Alternatively, plan meals that will be equally good packed in a picnic or eaten sitting round the TV if the weather or the mood changes. All the following recipes will fit the bill, from delicious flans and pies to mouthwatering crunchy coated chicken and a whole selection of totally transportable desserts.

## KNOW-HOW

The key to a good family picnic is to keep it simple. Avoid rich or messy food or anything that has a tendency to melt or be sticky. Choose items which can be eaten with the fingers if preferred. Remember to pack:

● Something to sit on – car rugs, blankets or towels and/or folding chairs for those who prefer to be off the ground.

● Crockery (preferably non-breakable picnicware) and a board or large plate on which to cut pies, filled loaves or French bread.

● Cutlery, including a sharp knife to cut any bread, pies, fruit and so on; at least one knife for spreading; spoons for serving, stirring tea, soup etc., and for eating any desserts.

● A cloth to spread the food out on.

● Clear, unbreakable tumblers for cold drinks and non-breakable cups for hot drinks.

● Paper napkins or kitchen paper (paper towels).

● Wet-wipes or damp, clean washing-up cloths or face flannels in a plastic bag to wipe sticky fingers.

## Top Tips

A pan of hot new potatoes tastes absolutely wonderful as an accompaniment to any picnic lunch. Simply boil them in your normal way and drain. Immediately put a clean tea towel (dish cloth) over them and replace the lid. Wrap the whole pan up in a towel or the car rug in the boot (trunk) and leave until ready to eat.

If you fancy warm French bread with your lunch, wrap it in foil. When you stop the car at your destination, lay the wrapped loaf on the radiator under the bonnet (hood). Turn the loaf over after about 5-10 minutes (don't forget a tub of butter or bread spread).

Whole baby salad vegetables are better on this type of picnic than sliced or chopped salads. Take a bag of washed cherry tomatoes, cleaned radishes and spring onions (scallions), baby sweetcorn (corn) cobs and sticks of raw carrot. Take a whole cucumber and cut it up at the meal time. Take a plastic box of washed but untorn salad leaves and pack any dressings separately.

Even if you're taking desserts, pack a selection of fresh fruit, and some cheese and biscuits – it's surprising how hungry people get in the open air!

An aerosol can of whipped cream is an easily transportable accompaniment to many of the desserts suggested (and ultra-popular with the children!).

The Fork Salads (see Everyday Outdoor Eating, page 120) also make great family picnic meals. Pack them in individual containers, take some crusty rolls and butter and fresh fruit and perhaps some sweet biscuits or a cake and you have a simple-to-eat feast. But don't forget to pack the forks!

# *Drinks*

Rather than taking vacuum flasks of tea or coffee, fill the flasks with boiling water and take instant coffee and tea (or bags) and a reclosable carton of milk. (Don't forget sugar, if you take it, and spoons.) You can take some sachets of instant soup or hot chocolate, too, in case the weather turns cold.

Individual cartons or plastic bottles of drink are more practical than cans for young children as they are less likely to spill if not drunk all at once. Avoid fizzy drinks for small children as they are more likely to make them feel car-sick on the return journey!

Cartons of wine are easier to pack than bottles and you don't need to remember a cork screw. You can now buy 1, 2 and 3 litre packs at many supermarkets. Remember to chill white wine in the fridge overnight, then pack it in a cool box with a cold pack. If you haven't got a cool box, put several news-papers in the freezer overnight and, just before leaving, use them to wrap the wine.

Then wrap in several more layers of unfrozen newspaper and put in a carrier bag. If you can't be bothered to pack glasses, buy individual ring-pull cans of wine.

Cold beers can be taken stored in exactly the same way. If you take small bottles rather than cans, remember the bottle opener (or choose bottles with screw-off caps). If you prefer a low-alcohol beer, check the labels. Many are still as much as 1 per cent alcohol by volume. Alternatively choose canned shandy or root beer.

Cider is a popular drink for picnics. It isn't vital that it's chilled and it is available in plastic bottles or cans which are better for transporting than glass. Sparkling apple juice is a refreshing, non-alcoholic alternative.

Freeze plastic bottles of still mineral water (with a little of the water poured off first to allow enough headroom). Pack normally. The water will thaw during the day but still be deliciously cold.

# Transportable Main Courses

## Blushing Beetroot Quiche

Try adding a drained 185 g/6½ oz/medium can of tuna to the beetroot and using only 175 g/6 oz each of beetroot and potato.

### SERVES 4

175 g/6 oz/1½ cups wholemeal flour

Pinch of salt

75 g/3 oz/⅓ cup hard margarine, cut into pieces

15 ml/1 tbsp caraway seeds

Cold water to mix

FILLING:

1 small red onion, finely chopped

15 g/½ oz/1 tbsp butter or margarine

225 g/8 oz cooked beetroot (red beets), diced

225 g/8 oz cooked new potatoes, diced

150 ml/¼ pt/⅔ cup soured (dairy sour) cream

150 ml/¼ pt/⅔ cup milk

2 eggs, beaten

Salt and freshly ground black pepper

5 ml/1 tsp dried summer savory

100 g/4 oz/1 cup Gruyère (Swiss) cheese, grated

15 ml/1 tbsp chopped parsley

TO SERVE:

Cucumber sticks

Baby sweetcorn (corn) cobs

**1**

Mix the flour and salt in a bowl. Add the margarine and rub in with the fingertips until the mixture resembles breadcrumbs. Stir in the caraway seeds and enough cold water to form a firm dough.

**2**

Knead gently on a lightly floured surface. Roll out and use to line a 20 cm/8 in flan tin (pie pan) set on a baking (cookie) sheet.

**3**

Fry (sauté) the onion in the butter or margarine for 2 minutes to soften. Stir in the beetroot and potato, then turn into the flan case (pie shell).

**4**

Beat the soured cream and milk with the eggs, a little salt and pepper and the summer savory and pour over the vegetables. Cover with the cheese and sprinkle with parsley. Bake in a preheated oven at 190°C/375°F/gas mark 5 for about 45 minutes until set and golden brown. Leave to cool. Wrap in foil. Serve with cucumber sticks and baby corn cobs.

# Cottage Cheese and Salmon Flan ❅

Mashed sardines or pilchards make an economical and tasty alternative to the salmon.

## SERVES 4

**1**

Sift the flour and salt into a bowl. Add the margarine and rub in with the fingertips until the mixture resembles breadcrumbs. Mix with enough cold water to form a firm dough.

**2**

Knead gently on a lightly floured surface. Roll out and use to line a 20 cm/8 in flan tin (pie pan).

**3**

Drain the salmon. Discard any bones and skin, then flake and mix with the mayonnaise, dill and chopped capers. Spread in the base of the flan case (pie shell).

**4**

Beat the egg, milk and cottage cheese together and season lightly. Pour into the flan and sprinkle with the chives. Bake in a preheated oven at 180°C/350°F/gas mark 4 for about 40 minutes until set. Leave to cool. Wrap in foil. Serve cold with coleslaw.

| SERVES 4 |
| --- |
| 175 g/6 oz/1½ cups plain (all-purpose) flour |
| Pinch of salt |
| 75 g/3 oz/⅓ cup hard margarine, cut into pieces |
| Cold water, to mix |
| FILLING: |
| 200 g/7 oz/1 small can of pink salmon |
| 10 ml/2 tsp mayonnaise |
| 2.5 ml/½ tsp dried dill (dill weed) |
| 5 ml/1 tsp capers, chopped |
| 1 egg |
| 150 ml/¼ pt/⅔ cup milk |
| 100 g/4 oz/½ cup cottage cheese |
| 15 ml/1 tbsp snipped chives |
| TO SERVE: |
| Coleslaw |

# Cheese and Vegetable Pie with Sage Pastry ✳

Sweet pickle or home-made fruit chutney goes well with this pie, which makes a satisfying meal for hearty outdoor appetites.

### SERVES 6

FILLING:

2 potatoes, thinly sliced

2 carrots, thinly sliced

1 bunch of spring onions (scallions), chopped

1 courgette (zucchini), thinly sliced

2 celery sticks, chopped

25 g/1 oz/2 tbsp butter or margarine

50 g/2 oz peas, frozen or fresh, shelled

175 g/6 oz/1½ cups Cheddar cheese, grated

Salt and freshly ground black pepper

SAGE PASTRY:

350 g/12 oz/3 cups plain (all-purpose) flour

1.5 ml/¼ tsp onion salt

175 g/6 oz/¾ cup hard margarine, cut into pieces

15 ml/1 tbsp finely chopped sage

Cold water to mix

TO FINISH:

2 eggs, beaten

150 ml/¼ pt/⅔ cup milk or single (light) cream

TO SERVE:

Baby pickled beetroot (red beets)

1

Prepare the filling. Gently fry (sauté) the potatoes, carrots, spring onions, courgette and celery in the butter or margarine for 5 minutes, stirring until softened but not browned. Leave to cool while making the pastry, then stir in the peas and the cheese and season to taste.

2

Sift the flour and onion salt into a bowl. Add the margarine and rub in with the fingertips until the mixture resembles fine breadcrumbs.

3

Stir in the sage and enough cold water to form a firm dough.

4

Knead gently on a lightly floured surface. Cut off about a quarter of the dough and reserve for a 'lid'. Roll out the remainder and use to line an 18 cm/7 in round, deep, loose-bottomed cake tin (pan), placed on a baking (cookie) sheet.

5

Spoon in the cooled cheese and vegetable mixture. Reserve 15 ml/1 tbsp of the beaten egg for glazing. Beat the milk or cream into the remainder. Pour into the pie.

**6**

Roll out the remaining pastry to a round for a lid. Brush the edges with water and place the lid in position. Crimp the edges between the finger and thumb and make a small hole in the centre of the pastry to allow the steam to escape. Makes 'leaves' and a 'rose' out of the pastry trimmings and use to decorate the pie. Brush with the reserved beaten egg to glaze.

**7**

Cook in a preheated oven at 200°C/400°F/gas mark 6 for 20 minutes, then reduce the heat to 180°C/350°F/gas mark 4 and continue cooking for a further 1¼ hours until the vegetables are tender. To test, push a skewer right down through the centre; if there is no resistance, you know the vegetables are cooked. Lay a piece of foil over the pastry if it is over-browning.

**8**

Leave to cool in the tin for at least 30 minutes, then gently loosen the edge with a round-bladed knife, if necessary. To remove the tin, place on top of a jam jar or can and carefully slide the tin down, leaving the pie on the base. Slide off the base, if liked, using a fish slice or palette knife, and cool on a wire rack. Wrap in foil. Serve cut into wedges with baby pickled beetroot.

---

**PICNIC PIES**

Pies of all kinds make great picnic dishes as they have their own pastry wrapping to hold everything together. You can transport them simply wrapped in foil, or you can leave them on the base of the tin for extra protection – or even inside the tin if you feel they may be damaged in transit.

# Oven-crunched Herb and Sesame Chicken

Ring the changes by simply using different flavoured stuffing mixes – there are lots available.

### SERVES 4

8 chicken legs

30 ml/2 tbsp plain (all-purpose) flour

85 g/3½ oz/1 packet of parsley, thyme and lemon stuffing mix

30 ml/2 tbsp sesame seeds

5 ml/1 tsp garlic salt

1 large egg, beaten

60 ml/4 tbsp sunflower oil

TO SERVE:

Salad-filled baguettes

**1**

Pull off and discard the skin from the chicken legs. Wipe them carefully with kitchen paper (paper towels), then dust the legs with flour.

**2**

Mix the stuffing with the sesame seeds and garlic salt.

**3**

Dip the legs in the beaten egg, then the stuffing mixture.

**4**

Pour the oil in a shallow baking tin (pan). Place the chicken legs in it. Bake in a preheated oven at 190°C/375°F/gas mark 5 for 20 minutes, turn over and cook on the other side for a further 20 minutes until crisp and golden. Drain on kitchen paper. Leave to cool. Place in an airtight container. Serve with salad-filled baguettes.

# Honey and Mint Lamb Cutlets

Substitute crushed rosemary or oregano for the mint, if you prefer. The longer you leave them to marinate, the better the flavour will be.

### 1
Trim any fat from the cutlets and cut off about 2.5 cm/1 in of meat from the ends of the bones. Place in a single layer in a shallow dish.

### 2
Whisk together the oil, vinegar, mint, honey and a little salt and pepper and pour over the cutlets. Leave to marinate for at least 1½ hours, turning from time to time.

### 3
Remove from the marinade and pat dry on kitchen paper (paper towels). Dust with flour and dip in beaten egg, then breadcrumbs to coat completely.

### 4
Heat a little oil in a large frying pan (skillet) and shallow-fry the cutlets for about 7 minutes on each side until golden brown and cooked through. Drain on kitchen paper and leave until cold.

### 5
Place a cutlet frill on the end of each bone, or wrap a strip of foil around. Store in an airtight container. Serve with watercress, tomato and mayonnaise rolls.

| SERVES 4 |
| --- |
| 8 lamb cutlets |
| 30 ml/2 tbsp olive oil |
| 15 ml/1 tbsp red wine vinegar |
| 15 ml/1 tbsp chopped mint |
| 5 ml/1 tsp clear honey |
| Salt and freshly ground black pepper |
| 20 ml/2 tbsp plain (all-purpose) flour |
| 2 eggs, beaten |
| 75 g/3 oz/1½ cups fresh breadcrumbs |
| Oil for shallow-frying |
| Cutlet frills or strips of foil |
| TO SERVE: |
| Tomato, watercress and mayonnaise rolls |

# Italian Sausage Loaf

Simple and inexpensive to make, this tasty and filling loaf is ideal for family meals and perfect for packed lunches too.

| SERVES 4 |
| --- |
| 295 g/10 oz/1 packet of bread mix |
| 15 ml/1 tbsp oil |
| 450 g/1 lb Italian pork sausages |
| 2 onions, thinly sliced |
| A little plain (all-purpose) flour |
| 30 ml/2 tbsp tomato relish |
| Beaten egg to glaze |
| 100 g/4 oz/½ cup butter, softened |
| 15 ml/1 tbsp Dijon mustard |
| 15 ml/1 tbsp finely chopped parsley |
| TO SERVE: |
| Cherry tomatoes |
| Cucumber sticks |

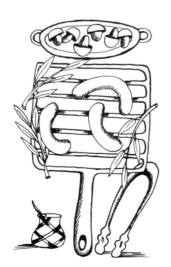

**1**
Make up the dough according to the packet directions, knead and leave until doubled in bulk as directed.

**2**
Meanwhile, heat the oil in a frying pan (skillet) and fry (sauté) the sausages until cooked through and browned all over. Drain on kitchen paper.

**3**
Add the onions to the pan and fry until soft and golden. Drain on kitchen paper.

**4**
Re-knead the dough and cut into three equal pieces.

**5**
Grease a 900 g/2 lb loaf tin (pan). Roll out one piece of the dough to fit the base of the tin, dust with flour and place in the tin. Dust the sausages with flour and lay four on top of the dough. Spread with the onions.

**6**
Roll out a second piece of dough, dust with flour and place on top of the onions. Add the remaining sausages and spread with the relish. Top with the third rolled-out piece of dough. Cover with clingfilm (plastic wrap) and leave in a warm place until the dough rises to the top of the tin. Brush with beaten egg and bake in a preheated oven at 220°C/425°F/gas mark 7 for 25 minutes or until golden brown and the base sounds

hollow when turned over and tapped. Cool on a wire rack. Wrap in foil.

**7**

Mash the butter with the mustard and parsley and pack in a small container. Cut the loaf into thick slices, spread with the mustard and parsley butter and serve with cherry tomatoes and cucumber sticks.

---

**SIMPLE ACCOMPANIMENTS**

Cherry tomatoes or little sticks of cucumber are perfect to pop into an airtight container and provide a juicy contrast to lots of foods.

---

# *Nutty Cheese and Vegetable Loaf* *

For vegetarians, line the loaf tin (pan) with green cabbage leaves, blanched for 2 minutes in boiling water.

**1**

Stretch the bacon rashers with the back of a knife and use to line an oiled 900 g/2 lb loaf tin, leaving the ends hanging slightly over the edge.

**2**

Mix all the remaining ingredients except the egg and milk together in a bowl, seasoning lightly. Beat the egg and milk together and stir in to bind.

**3**

Turn into the prepared tin and level the surface. Fold over the ends of the bacon. Cover with foil and bake in a preheated oven at 190°C/375°F/gas mark 5 for about 1½ hours until firm. Leave to cool in the tin. Wrap in clean foil to transport. Turn out on to a plate or board and serve cut into slices with extra chutney and a selection of salad stuffs.

| SERVES 6 |
| --- |
| 175 g/6 oz streaky bacon rashers (slices), rinded |
| Oil for greasing |
| 100 g/4 oz/1 cup peanuts and raisins, roughly chopped |
| 1 onion, finely chopped |
| 1 carrot, finely chopped |
| 1 small parsnip, finely chopped |
| 100 g/4 oz/2 cups fresh breadcrumbs |
| 175 g/6 oz/1½ cups Red Leicester cheese, grated |
| 20 ml/4 tsp curried fruit chutney |
| 15 ml/1 tbsp chopped parsley |
| Salt and freshly ground black pepper |
| 1 egg |
| 150 ml/¼ pt/⅔ cup milk |
| TO SERVE: |
| Extra chutney |
| Selection of salad stuffs |

# Blue Cheese and Sun-dried Tomato Slice

For a quick alternative, instead of the soft blue cheese, mashed with butter and fromage frais, use about 225 g/8 oz cheese spread, sprinkled with the carrot.

## SERVES 4–6

800 g/1¾ lb/1 large uncut wholemeal loaf

175 g/6 oz/¾ cup butter, softened

175 g/6 oz soft blue cheese

1 carrot, grated

30 ml/2 tbsp fromage frais

2 sun-dried tomatoes in oil, drained and finely chopped

15 ml/1 tbsp snipped chives

6 tomatoes, sliced

5 ml/1 tsp dried dill (dill weed)

3 dill pickles, sliced

TO SERVE:

Radishes

Celery sticks

**1**

Cut the loaf horizontally into seven slices. Lay them on a work surface and spread each slice with a very little of the butter.

**2**

Mash the blue cheese with the carrot and half the remaining butter until well blended. Work in the fromage frais.

**3**

Mash the remaining butter with the sun-dried tomatoes and chives.

**4**

Spread the base slice of bread with a third of the blue cheese mixture and top with some of the sliced tomatoes. Sprinkle with a little dill.

**5**

Spread the next with a third of the tomato butter and top with dill pickle slices. Repeat the layers, then re-shape the loaf and top with the buttered crust.

**6**

Wrap tightly in foil and chill for at least 1 hour.

**7**

Carefully cut into thick slices to serve with radishes and celery sticks.

# Turkey and Mushroom Bloomer

You can, of course, use chicken instead of turkey in this recipe, which keeps deliciously moist inside its golden crusty shell.

### 1

Cut a slice horizontally off the loaf, about a third of the way from the top. Pull out most of the soft bread, leaving a crust 'shell'. Melt a third of the butter or margarine and use to brush the inside of the loaf and the cut side of the lid.

### 2

Melt half the remaining butter in a saucepan. Fry (sauté) the onion for 2 minutes, stirring, until softened but not browned. Stir in the carrots and mushrooms and fry for a further 1 minute, stirring. Remove from the heat.

### 3

Make the pulled-out bread into breadcrumbs and add to the onion mixture with the turkey. Mix together well and season with the herbs, salt and pepper. Mix with the beaten egg to bind.

### 4

Press half the mixture into the bread shell. Lay the three hard-boiled eggs along the centre, then top with the remaining meat mixture. Press down lightly, then place the lid on top.

### 5

Melt the remaining butter and brush all over the loaf. Wrap in foil and bake in a preheated oven at 190°C/375°F/gas mark 5 for 1¼ hours until cooked through. Open the foil for the last 15 minutes of cooking to crisp. Leave to cool. Rewrap for transporting. Serve cut into thick slices with pickles.

| SERVES 4–6 |
| --- |
| 1 small bloomer loaf |
| 75 g/3 oz/⅓ cup butter or margarine |
| 1 onion, finely chopped |
| 2 carrots, grated |
| 100 g/4 oz button mushrooms, sliced |
| 225 g/8 oz minced (ground) raw turkey |
| 5 ml/1 tsp dried thyme |
| 15 ml/1 tbsp chopped parsley |
| Salt and freshly ground black pepper |
| 1 egg, beaten |
| 3 hard-boiled (hard-cooked) eggs |
| TO SERVE: |
| Pickles |

# Stuffed Pork Roll with Mortadella

This is also good made with boned, lean breast of lamb and garlic sausage instead of Mortadella, and is equally delicious served hot as a roast.

### SERVES 6

1.5 kg/3 lb piece of thin end of belly pork

Salt and freshly ground black pepper

4 slices of Mortadella sausage

2 spring onions (scallions), finely chopped

½ small red (bell) pepper, diced

45 ml/3 tbsp frozen sweetcorn (corn)

30 ml/2 tbsp cooked long-grain rice

2.5 ml/½ tsp dried mixed herbs

1 small egg, beaten

A little oil

TO SERVE:

Apple chutney

Green salad

**1**

Remove the bones from the pork, then score the rind into thin strips with a sharp knife (or ask the butcher to do this for you).

**2**

Season the meat with a little salt and pepper, then lay the slices of Mortadella on top. Mix the spring onions, pepper, corn and rice together and season lightly. Mix in the herbs, then enough of the beaten egg to bind.

**3**

Spread the mixture over the pork. Roll up and tie securely in several places with string.

**4**

Place on a rack in a roasting tin (pan) and rub the skin with oil and a little salt. Roast in a preheated oven at 190°C/375°F/gas mark 5 for 2 hours. Remove from the roasting tin and leave to cool. Remove the string and wrap in foil. Serve cut into thick slices with apple chutney and a green salad.

# Individual Stuffed Breads

**B**aguettes, pittas, bagels, tortillas and naans are all delicious vehicles for tasty fillings. To prepare, simply split baguettes or bagels, not quite through, and butter, if liked. Cut pittas in half and open up each half to make a pocket or leave whole and split along one edge to make a pocket. Naans and tortillas are best spread with the chosen filling and then rolled up. Try any of the following:

**Chillied Egg:** Chop hard-boiled (hard-cooked) egg, moisten with mayonnaise and flavour to taste with fresh, chopped green chilli. For extra 'bite', add a layer of mustard and cress and some thinly sliced onion.

**Greek Goddess:** Spread the bread with taramasalata or hummus. Sprinkle with lemon juice. Add shredded lettuce, sliced tomato and cucumber, thinly sliced onion, a few chopped black olives and some crumbled Feta cheese.

**Brunch Special:** Fry (sauté) chopped bacon or sausages in a little butter in a frying pan (skillet). Make into an omelette with beaten eggs. Season to taste, fold and leave to cool. Spread the bread with tomato ketchup (catsup) or brown sauce. Add the omelette and top with sliced tomato and/or a few slices of raw mushroom.

**Curried Veggibite:** Mash canned pease pudding with mango chutney and curry paste to taste. Spread on the bread. Sprinkle with lemon juice. Top with shredded lettuce, chopped cucumber, a dollop of thick plain yoghurt and a sprinkling of dried mint.

**Pâté Potential:** Spread the bread with a very little Dijon mustard. Fill with thin slices of coarse liver pâté, slices of gherkin (cornichon) and tomato and a little chopped spring onion (scallion). Add some curly endive (frisée lettuce) leaves.

**Crabstick Cocktail:** Chop the crabsticks. Mix with a little mayonnaise and flavour with tomato ketchup (catsup), Worcestershire sauce, cayenne and a little salt and pepper. Sharpen with lemon or lime juice, if liked. Put some shredded lettuce in the bread. Top with the crabstick mixture and add some slices of green (bell) pepper for crunchiness.

**Smokey Joe:** Cut skinned, ready-to-eat smoked mackerel fillets into slices. Flavour a little mayonnaise with horseradish sauce, lemon juice and black pepper. Spread on the bread, then fill with the mackerel. Top with slices of cucumber and radishes.

# Chocolate Walnut Cups

For a different but equally tempting treat, try using coconut-flavoured biscuits (cookies) instead of rich tea and desiccated (shredded) coconut instead of walnuts.

### SERVES 6

225 g/8 oz plain (semi-sweet) chocolate, broken into pieces

600 ml/1 pt/2½ cups milk

100 g/4 oz rich tea biscuits, finely crushed

2 eggs, separated

50 g/2 oz/½ cup walnut halves, chopped

TO SERVE:

Whipped cream (optional)

**1**

Reserve two squares of the chocolate and put the rest with the milk in a saucepan. Heat gently until the chocolate has completely melted, stirring all the time.

**2**

Stir in the biscuit crumbs and the egg yolks and stir until thickened.

**3**

Remove from the heat and leave to cool slightly. Whisk the egg whites until stiff and fold into the chocolate mixture with three-quarters of the chopped nuts.

**4**

Turn into six individual moulds or cups and stand in a roasting tin (pan) containing 1 cm/½ in hot water. Bake in a preheated oven at 180°C/350°F/gas mark 4 for about 20 minutes or until set. Leave to cool. Grate the remaining chocolate, mix with the remaining nuts and sprinkle over. Wrap in clingfilm (plastic wrap) and chill until ready to pack. Serve with whipped cream, if liked.

# Fresh Cherry and Almond Bake ❆

This is also delicious made with fresh apricots or greengages, when they are in season.

**1**

Sift the flour into a bowl. Add the butter or margarine and rub in with the fingertips until the mixture resembles breadcrumbs.

**2**

Stir in two-thirds of the sugar. Add the beaten egg, almond essence and enough milk or cream to form a soft dropping consistency.

**3**

Turn the mixture into a greased 18 cm/7 in square sandwich tin (pan), lined with non-stick baking parchment. Level the surface and cover with the cherries and almonds. Sprinkle with the remaining sugar.

**4**

Bake in a preheated oven at 180°C/350°F/gas mark 4 for about 40 minutes, until the cake springs back when lightly pressed. Leave until lukewarm, then take out of the tin, remove the paper and leave to cool completely on a wire rack. Store in an airtight container. Serve cut into squares with whipped cream, if liked.

| MAKES AN 18 CM/7 IN SQUARE CAKE |
| --- |
| 100 g/4 oz/1 cup self-raising (self-rising) flour |
| 50 g/2 oz/¼ cup butter or margarine, cut into pieces |
| 75 g/3 oz/⅓ cup light brown sugar |
| 1 egg, beaten |
| 2.5 ml/½ tsp almond essence (extract) |
| 30 ml/2 tbsp milk or single (light) cream |
| 225 g/8 oz red cherries, halved and stoned (pitted) |
| 15 ml/1 tbsp flaked (slivered) almonds |
| TO SERVE: |
| Whipped cream (optional) |

# Rhubarb and Redcurrant Fingers

These fingers make perfect picnic food – simple to make, easy to transport and delicious to eat.

## MAKES 18

6 sticks of rhubarb

225 g/8 oz/2 cups plain (all-purpose) flour

100 g/4 oz/½ cup hard margarine, cut into pieces

50 g/2 oz/¼ cup caster (superfine) sugar

1 egg, separated

Cold water

30 ml/2 tbsp redcurrant jelly (clear conserve)

TO SERVE:

Individual pots of custard or plain yoghurt

**1**

Scrub and trim the rhubarb to 30 cm/12 in sticks. Discard any that are wooden or stringy; young, tender rhubarb is best.

**2**

Put the flour in a bowl and rub in the margarine until the mixture resembles breadcrumbs. Stir in 25 g/ 1 oz/2 tbsp of the sugar. Mix with the egg yolk and enough water to form a firm dough.

**3**

Knead gently on a lightly floured surface and roll out to a 46 × 33 cm/18 × 13 in rectangle. Brush with the redcurrant jelly. Cut the pastry into six equal lengths, 7.5 cm/3 in wide.

**4**

Place a rhubarb stick on top of each. Fold the pastry over and press the edges well together to seal. Knock up with the back of a knife and transfer to a lightly greased baking (cookie) sheet.

**5**

Brush with the lightly beaten egg white, then sprinkle with the remaining sugar. Bake in a preheated oven at 200°C/400°F/gas mark 6 for about 20–25 minutes until golden brown and the rhubarb is tender.

**6**

Leave to cool, then cut each stick into three pieces. Transport in an airtight container.

*Opposite: Spinach and Smoked Salmon Rolls (page 37)*

# Chocolate Lattice Box Cake ✳

Substitute hazelnuts for the cherries for a change; reserve a few whole ones for decoration and chop the remainder.

### 1

Reserve 25 g/1 oz of the chocolate and melt the remainder in a pan with the butter or margarine and the syrup.

### 2

Stir in the biscuit crumbs with the sultanas. Chop two-thirds of the cherries and add. Cut off a third of the almond paste and reserve. Chop the remainder and add to the pan. Mix well.

### 3

Oil an 18 cm/7 in loose-bottomed cake tin (pan) and line the base with non-stick baking parchment. Press in the crumb mixture.

### 4

Roll out the reserved almond paste thinly and cut into 12 thin strips. Lay in a lattice pattern on top of the cake, trimming to fit. Dot the remaining halved glacé cherries in some of the spaces. Wrap in clingfilm (plastic wrap). Chill until firm. Remove from the tin when ready to serve, cut into wedges.

**MAKES AN 18 CM/7 IN SQUARE CAKE**

200 g/7 oz plain (semi-sweet) chocolate

175 g/6 oz/¾ cup butter or margarine

45 ml/3 tbsp golden (light corn) syrup

225 g/8 oz digestive biscuits (graham crackers), crushed

50 g/2 oz/½ cup sultanas (golden raisins)

75 g/3 oz/¾ cup glacé (candied) cherries, halved

176 g/6 oz white almond paste

Oil for greasing

*Opposite: Fragrant Herb Poussins with Lemon and Honey (page 46)*

# Lemon and Mint Ice Cream✳

This is a luxurious dessert. For a version suitable for young children, use a large can of chilled evaporated milk, whisked with the sugar, instead of the eggs.

### SERVES 4–6

4 eggs, separated

100 g/4 oz/½ cup caster (superfine) sugar

300 ml/½ pt/1¼ cups double (heavy) cream

Finely grated rind and juice of 2 lemons

7.5 ml/1½ tsp dried mint

**1**

Whisk the egg whites until stiff. Whisk in 25 g/1 oz/2 tbsp of the sugar and continue whisking until stiff. Repeat until all the sugar is incorporated.

**2**

Lightly beat the egg yolks and fold in with a metal spoon.

**3**

Whip the cream with the lemon rind, juice and mint until softly peaking. Fold the egg mixture into the lemon cream with a metal spoon.

**4**

Turn into a metal container and freeze until half-firm (about 2 hours). Whisk with a fork until smooth, then freeze again until firm. When ready to pack, allow to soften for about 10 minutes before scooping into a chilled, wide-necked vacuum flask for transporting.

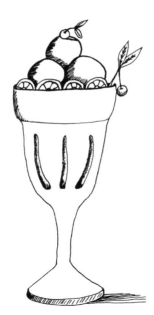

# Muscovado Coffee Creams

If you are not a coffee lover, use vanilla essence (extract), to taste, instead of the coffee granules and decorate with grated chocolate.

**1**

*B*ring the milk and cream just to the boil in a saucepan. Do not allow the mixture to boil fully, or it will curdle when you add it to the eggs.

**2**

Whisk the eggs, egg yolks, sugar and coffee granules together in a bowl until well blended. Stir in the hot milk and cream and whisk well.

**3**

Strain into six individual dishes. Place in a roasting tin (pan) containing 1 cm/½ in hot water. Cover the dishes with foil and bake in a preheated oven at 160°C/ 325°F/gas mark 3 for about 40 minutes or until set. Remove from the tin and leave to cool. Top each with three chocolate coffee beans, if liked, and wrap in clingfilm (plastic wrap). Chill until needed.

| SERVES 6 |
| --- |
| 300 ml/½ pt/1¼ cups milk |
| 300 ml/½ pt/1¼ cups single (light) cream |
| 2 eggs |
| 2 egg yolks |
| 30 ml/2 tbsp light muscovado sugar |
| 15 ml/1 tbsp instant coffee granules |
| TO DECORATE: |
| 18 chocolate coffee beans (optional) |

# Butterscotch-frosted Carrot Cake

For an unusual alternative, use two parsnips instead of the carrots and 5 ml/1 tsp mixed (apple-pie) spice instead of the orange rind.

### MAKES A 20 CM/8 IN ROUND CAKE

50 g/2 oz/½ cup self-raising (self-rising) flour

2.5 ml/½ tsp mixed (apple-pie) spice

100 g/4 oz/½ cup butter or margarine

100 g/4 oz/½ cup light brown sugar

2 eggs, separated

3 large carrots, grated

50 g/2 oz/½ cup ground almonds

Grated rind of 1 orange

FROSTING:

100 g/4 oz/½ cup butter or margarine

200 g/7 oz/scant 1 cup light brown sugar

90 ml/6 tbsp milk

175 g/6 oz/¾ cup icing (confectioners') sugar, sifted

**1**

Put the flour and spice in a bowl and rub in 25 g/1 oz/2 tbsp of the butter or margarine until the mixture resembles breadcrumbs.

**2**

Whisk the sugar and egg yolks with an electric beater until thick and pale. Stir in the carrots, ground almonds and orange rind. Fold in the flour mixture.

**3**

Whisk the egg whites until stiff and fold in with a metal spoon. Turn into a 20 cm/8 in deep round cake tin (pan), greased and base-lined.

**4**

Bake in a preheated oven at 180°C/350°F/gas mark 4 for about 45 minutes until risen and golden. Cool slightly, turn out, remove the paper and leave to cool.

**5**

To make the frosting, melt the butter or margarine with the brown sugar. Boil, stirring, for 2 minutes. Stir in the milk. Remove from the heat and cool until lukewarm. Beat in the icing sugar, a little at a time.

**6**

Split the cake in half horizontally. Sandwich the halves together with about half of the frosting. Spread the remainder over the top and ripple with the prongs of a fork. Store in an airtight container.

# Fruity Kebabs with Yoghurt Dip

Ring the changes with other seasonal fruits of your choice.

Thread the fruits on to eight cocktail sticks (toothpicks). Pack in a rigid container. At the picnic, each person sprinkles a few pistachio nuts in their pot of yoghurt and dips in the fruit kebabs.

### SERVES 4

8 small strawberries

4 apricots, halved and stoned (pitted)

4 greengages, halved and stoned

4 red plums, halved and stoned

30 ml/2 tbsp chopped pistachio nuts

4 individual pots of Greek-style
  yoghurt with honey

# Blackcurrant Mallow

This can be made with other soft canned fruits, such as raspberries or strawberries.

**1**

Drain the juice from the blackcurrants and measure 60 ml/4 tbsp of it into a saucepan. Add the marshmallows and stir gently over a low heat until melted.

**2**

Remove from the heat and stir in the drained blackcurrants. When well blended, turn into four individual containers and chill until set.

**3**

Decorate each with a crystallised violet or angelica 'leaves', if liked, then cover in clingfilm (plastic wrap) or with lids to transport.

### SERVES 4

400 g/14 oz/1 large can of
  blackcurrants in natural juice

250 g/9 oz marshmallows, snipped
  with scissors if large

TO DECORATE:

Crystallised (candied) violets or
  angelica 'leaves' (optional)

# Golden Dutch Apple and Lemon Cake

The apple makes this cake deliciously moist. Omit the lemon and dust with ground cinnamon, if you prefer.

**MAKES A 28 × 18 CM/11 × 7 IN SLAB CAKE**

2 eggs

250 g/9 oz/good 1 cup caster (superfine) sugar

100 g/4 oz/½ cup butter or margarine

150 ml/¼ pt/⅔ cup milk

15 ml/1 tbsp dried milk powder (non-fat dry milk)

175 g/6 oz/1½ cups self-raising (self-rising) flour

5 ml/1 tsp baking powder

4 cooking (tart) apples, peeled, cored and sliced

Grated rind of 1 lemon

**1**

Whisk the eggs and all but 30 ml/2 tbsp of the sugar in a bowl until thick and very pale yellow.

**2**

Heat the butter or margarine and milk in a saucepan until the fat melts. Whisk in the milk powder. Bring to the boil and stir into the eggs and sugar.

**3**

Sift the flour and baking powder over the surface and fold in with a metal spoon.

**4**

Pour into a greased and floured 28 × 18 cm/11 × 7 in shallow baking tin (pan).

**5**

Lay the slices of apple over the surface. Mix the remaining sugar with the lemon rind and sprinkle over.

**6**

Bake in a preheated oven at 200°C/400°F/gas mark 6 for 25 minutes until golden brown and the centre springs back when lightly pressed. Leave to cool in the tin, then loosen. Wrap and transport in the tin. Serve cut into squares.

# Hampers with Style

Have you ever longed to order a picnic hamper from Fortnum's or Harrods? Imagine opening the lid of the enormous wicker crate to find such exotica as quails' egg tartlets, fragrant herb poussins richly glazed with lemon and honey and fresh figs served with individual goats' cheeses coated in pistachio nuts. Well, you can create these and many more exquisite dishes at a fraction of the cost of ordering an elegant picnic from London. So if you are planning a trip to Henley Regatta, to Glyndebourne or simply a private party in the country for a very special occasion, then you'll find everything you need in this chapter. Oh, and although wicker is aesthetically pleasing, cool boxes are much more practical!

## KNOW-HOW

If you are planning a really stylish picnic, then you have to set the scene. You will need:

- Enough tables and chairs for everyone to sit and eat comfortably, plus at least one other table (preferably two) for laying out the food and drinks.

- Table cloths and napkins.

- Small, low, central table decorations. Silk flowers are best because they won't wilt if the sun is hot and they won't be damaged *en route*.

- Garden umbrellas or a large awning to create shade.

- Crockery (including coffee and tea cups for after the meal).

- Silver (or good-quality stainless steel) cutlery (including plenty of serving spoons, slices and so on).

- Cruet sets.

- Aperitif, wine and water glasses (avoid any with very long stems as they are more likely to topple over).

- Wine coolers.

- To complete the scene – hire a butler!

## Top Tips

If you want to use fresh herbs as a garnish (as suggested in several of the recipes), take them growing in a pot rather than already cut (they are very cheap to buy in the supermarket). That way they will stay fresh.

To prevent salad leaves wilting en route, pack in a salad crisper. If you don't possess one, put the prepared leaves in a plastic bag. Hold the neck of the bag over the nozzle of a hair-dryer. Switch to cold air and fill the bag with air. Tie up securely with a bag twist and transport.

Take hot potatoes as for a family picnic (see page 8) but toss in butter and add a good sprinkling of chopped parsley or snipped chives before transporting.

You can include soups in a hamper meal or picnic if you transport them in a wide-necked vacuum flask.

# Drinks

When you all assemble before the meal, you will want to offer some refreshment. A good pre-lunch drink would be:

- Bucks Fizz – champagne or other sparkling wine and orange juice.

- Kir – blackcurrant liqueur and dry white wine.

- Kir Royale – blackcurrant liqueur with sparkling wine.

- Pimms.

For a non-alcoholic alternative, try:

- Sparkling fruit cup – mixed pineapple, orange and cranberry juices, topped up with lemonade or sparkling mineral water.

- Black Watch – a little blackcurrant cordial, blended with red grape juice and topped up with sparkling mineral water.

- Sunset – pour about 2.5 cm/1 in grenadine syrup over lots of ice in tall glasses. Slowly top up with orange juice. Do not stir.

It is important that all these drinks are properly chilled. Pack a whole cool box of ice (you can often buy it from your local off-licence or wine merchant or in large bags from your supermarket or freezer centre). Pimms needs garnishing – lots of cucumber slices, orange and lemon slices and, ideally, borage, or if not available use mint. Prepare in advance and take in an airtight container. Don't forget a large jug to mix it in – and the lemonade to top up the Pimms base.

## With the meal

Serve whatever wines you like, and stick to one for simplicity if you prefer. But if you want to go the whole hog, choose a dry white for any fish, light dishes or white meats and serve red with red meats, game and highly flavoured dishes. For dessert, choose a sweet white (still or sparkling). If you are planning to offer a cheese course as well, then serve port or more red wine.

Have plenty of still or sparkling mineral water available too, and non-alcoholic alternatives for those who do not drink (or are driving). I recommend red or white grape juice in preference to de-alcoholised wine.

## After the meal

Coffee or tea can be offered. As for any picnic, if you haven't got heating facilities, take boiling water in vacuum flasks and ground or instant coffee and tea bags. Don't forget cream and/or milk and sugar.

# Opulent Openers

## Parma Ham and Melon Salad

Any raw, cured ham can be used for this refreshing and unusual salad.

### SERVES 6

3 small galia or cantaloupe melons, halved and seeded

75 g/3 oz Parma ham, cut into thin strips

100 g/4 oz Mozzarella, cut into small dice

12 cherry tomatoes, halved

12 basil leaves, torn

Olive oil

White wine vinegar

Freshly ground black pepper

TO GARNISH:

6 small sprigs of basil

**1**

Scoop out the melon using a melon baller or cut into cubes. Mix with the ham, cheese, tomatoes and torn basil leaves.

**2**

Spoon into the melon shells and pack in an airtight container. Chill.

**3**

When about to serve, transfer the melon halves to small bowls. Drizzle with oil and vinegar and add a good grinding of black pepper. Garnish each with a small sprig of basil and serve.

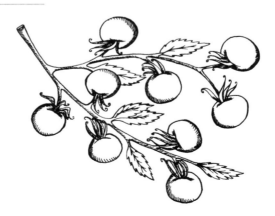

# Spinach and Smoked Salmon Rolls *

Use garlic and herb soft cheese instead of making the flavoured cheese mixture if you are in a hurry! See photograph on page 25.

**1**

Trim the stalks from the spinach and plunge the leaves into boiling water for 1 minute. Drain, rinse with cold water and drain again. Pat dry on kitchen paper (paper towels).

**2**

Mash the cheese with the herbs, lemon and anchovy essence. Season to taste with pepper. Stir in the milk to thin slightly.

**3**

Cut the smoked salmon slices in half lengthways. Spread each piece gently with the cheese mixture. Carefully roll up. Lay each on a spinach leaf, fold in the sides, then roll up tightly. Place in an airtight container and chill until ready to pack.

**4**

Put the dressing ingredients in a screw-topped jar. Shake well. To serve, put two rolls on each of six serving plates. Cut into attractive slices. Garnish with salad leaves. Shake the dressing and spoon a little over the slices before serving.

| SERVES 6 |
| --- |
| 12 spinach leaves |
| 200 g/7 oz/scant 1 cup medium-fat soft cheese |
| 15 ml/1 tbsp chopped parsley |
| 15 ml/1 tbsp chopped dill (dill weed) |
| Finely grated rind of 1 lemon |
| 10 ml/2 tsp anchovy essence (extract) |
| Freshly ground black pepper |
| 15 ml/1 tbsp milk |
| 6 slices of smoked salmon |
| DRESSING: |
| 45 ml/3 tbsp olive oil |
| 15 ml/1 tbsp lemon juice |
| 5 ml/1 tsp balsamic vinegar |
| 2.5 ml/$\frac{1}{2}$ tsp caster (superfine) sugar |
| 15 ml/1 tbsp chopped dill |
| Freshly ground black pepper |
| Salt |
| TO GARNISH: |
| A few mixed salad leaves |

# Quails' Egg Tartlets

If you can't get quails' eggs, use half a small hen's egg for the centre of each tartlet.

### SERVES 6

150 ml/¼ pt/⅔ cup boiling water

1 chicken stock cube

10 ml/2 tsp powdered gelatine

150 g/5 oz/1¼ cups wholemeal flour

Pinch of salt

65 g/2½ oz/scant ⅓ cup butter, cut into pieces

Cold water to mix

FILLING:

6 quails' eggs

75 g/3 oz smooth chicken liver pâté

75 g/3 oz/⅓ cup medium-fat soft cheese

15 ml/1 tbsp brandy

1 egg white

Salt and freshly ground black pepper

12 black olives, stoned (pitted)

12 green olives, stoned

6 small sprigs of parsley

1

Pour the boiling water on to the stock cube in a measuring jug. Stir until dissolved. Sprinkle on the gelatine and stir until completely dissolved. Leave to cool until the consistency of egg white.

2

Meanwhile, mix the flour and salt in a bowl. Add the butter and rub in with the fingertips. Mix with enough cold water to form a firm dough. Knead gently on a lightly floured surface. Use to line six individual flan rings set on a baking (cookie) sheet. Prick the bases with a fork and line with crumpled foil. Bake in a preheated oven at 200°C/400°F/gas mark 6 for 10 minutes, remove the foil and return to the oven for 5 minutes to dry out. Remove from the oven and leave to cool.

3

Place the eggs in a pan and cover with cold water. Bring to the boil, cook for 3 minutes, then drain and cover with cold water. When cold, remove the shells.

4

Beat the pâté with the cheese and brandy until smooth. Whisk the egg white until stiff and fold into the mixture with a metal spoon. Season to taste.

5

Spoon the pâté into the pastry cases (shells). Put a quail's egg on the centre of each. Arrange the olives around. Spoon the almost-jellied stock over, garnish each with a sprig of parsley and chill. Transport in an airtight container.

# Mediterranean Aubergines ✳

Try using large courgettes (zucchini) instead of aubergines (eggplants) for a change.

**1**

Trim off the stalks from the aubergines. Boil in lightly salted water for 10 minutes. Drain and plunge in cold water. When cool enough to handle, drain and cut in half lengthways.

**2**

Scoop out most of the flesh, leaving the 'shells' intact. Chop the flesh and reserve.

**3**

Brush a baking tin (pan) with oil. Lay the shells in it and brush each with a little more oil. Season with salt and pepper. Bake in a preheated oven at 180°C/350°F/ gas mark 4 for 30 minutes. Remove from the oven.

**4**

Meanwhile, heat 45 ml/3 tbsp of oil in a saucepan. Add the onion and garlic and fry (sauté), stirring, for 3 minutes to soften.

**5**

Add all the remaining ingredients except the parsley. Bring to the boil and simmer for 10 minutes until the onions are soft and the mixture is bathed in sauce. Season to taste and leave to cool.

**6**

Spoon into the aubergine shells. Sprinkle with parsley, place in a large airtight container and chill until ready to pack.

| SERVES 6 |
| --- |
| 3 even-sized aubergines |
| Salt and freshly ground black pepper |
| Olive oil |
| 2 Spanish onions, chopped |
| 1 garlic clove, crushed |
| 150 ml/¼ pt/⅔ cup passata (sieved tomatoes) |
| 5 ml/1 tsp caster (superfine) sugar |
| 30 ml/2 tbsp pine nuts |
| 50 g/2 oz/1 can of anchovy fillets, drained and chopped |
| 12 black olives, stoned (pitted) and chopped |
| 5 ml/1 tsp ground cinnamon |
| 15 ml/1 tbsp chopped parsley |

# Crusted Prawn and Avocado Mousse

If you don't feel like making the bread case, simply make the mousse in a soufflé dish and top it with the prawn and gelatine mixture.

| SERVES 6-8 |
| --- |

**MOUSSE:**

25 g/1 oz/2 tbsp powdered gelatine

150 ml/¼ pt/⅔ cup very hot chicken stock

30 ml/2 tbsp dry vermouth

175 g/6 oz cooked, peeled prawns (shrimp)

5 thin slices of lemon

2 ripe avocados, stoned (pitted)

15 ml/1 tbsp lemon juice

1.5 ml/¼ tbsp Tabasco sauce

15 ml/1 tbsp Worcestershire sauce

15 ml/1 tbsp anchovy essence (extract)

15 ml/1 tbsp grated onion

3 eggs, separated

150 ml/¼ pt/⅔ cup mayonnaise

150 ml/¼ pt/⅔ cup whipping cream, whipped

Salt and freshly ground black pepper

**CASE:**

6 slices of white bread, crusts removed

75 g/3 oz/⅓ cup butter

**TO GARNISH:**

Sprigs of parsley

**1**

Dissolve the gelatine in the stock. Spoon 30 ml/2 tbsp into the base of an oiled 18 cm/7 in round soufflé dish. Stir in the vermouth and 30 ml/2 tbsp of water.

**2**

Arrange eight prawns attractively in the liquid with the lemon slices. Leave to set.

**3**

Meanwhile, mash the avocados with 10 ml/2 tsp of the lemon juice until smooth. Beat in the Tabasco and Worcestershire sauces, the anchovy essence, onion and egg yolks. Chop the remaining prawns and add. Stir in the remaining gelatine mixture, then the mayonnaise and cream. Finally, whisk the egg whites until stiff and fold in with a metal spoon. Season to taste. Spoon into the prepared dish and chill until set.

**4**

Brush the bread with melted butter to coat both sides completely. Use five slices to line a 20 cm/8 in loose-bottomed flan tin (pie pan) with a corner of each slice pointing up out of the tin. Press the final slice into the base. Press down well and bake in a preheated oven at 190°C/375°F/gas mark 5 for about 25 minutes until crisp and golden brown. Remove from the oven and leave to cool. Place on the upturned lid of an airtight container that you can use to transport it.

**5**

Stand the base of the soufflé dish of mousse in hot water for 30 seconds. Invert over the baked case and, holding the container lid and dish, give a firm shake to loosen the mousse. Lift off the soufflé dish. Invert the airtight container over the mousse and seal on to the upturned lid. Transport carefully so it cannot slide about. Transfer to a serving plate and garnish with parsley before serving.

**TRANSPORT SOLUTIONS**

**You can use an upturned airtight container to transport all kinds of foods, from mousses to cakes. Seal the container carefully, then simply remove the main part and your recipe is ready on its own plate.**

# Crab and Camembert Parcels *

These are also delicious served hot, and make perfect starters for a dinner party.

**1**

*L*ay the sheets of filo pastry on the work surface and brush with a little melted butter. Fold in half widthways and brush with a little more butter.

**2**

Put a pile of crabmeat in the centre of each piece of pastry. Cut the cheese wedges in half horizontally and lay two pieces over each pile of crab. Spoon on the crème fraîche. Sprinkle with dill and season lightly. Fold the pastry over the filling to form parcels.

**3**

Transfer to a lightly buttered baking (cookie) sheet and brush with a little more butter. Bake in a preheated oven at 190°C/375°F/gas mark 5 for about 15 minutes until crisp and golden. Leave to cool.

**4**

Arrange on serving plates with a few salad leaves and avocado slices on one side. Spoon 10 ml/2 tsp French dressing over each garnish and serve.

**SERVES 6**

6 rectangular sheets of filo pastry (paste)

Melted butter for brushing

2 × 200 g/7 oz/small cans of white crabmeat

1 round Camembert, cut into 6 wedges

90 ml/6 tbsp crème fraîche

30 ml/2 tbsp dried dill (dill weed)

Salt and freshly ground black pepper

TO GARNISH:

Salad leaves

2 small avocados, sliced and tossed in lemon juice

60 ml/4 tbsp French dressing

# Stylish Chilled Soups

## Chilled Consommé with 'Caviare'

If you don't like lumpfish roe, top the soured (dairy sour) cream with finely chopped green and red (bell) pepper.

| SERVES 6 |
| --- |
| 3 × 295 g/10½ oz/medium cans of concentrated beef consommé |
| 60 ml/4 tbsp medium sherry |
| A few drops of Tabasco sauce |
| 1 small carton of soured cream |
| 50 g/2 oz/1 small jar of Danish lumpfish roe |

**1**

Empty the contents of the cans of consommé into a bowl. Stir in the sherry and Tabasco and chill until jellied.

**2**

To serve, spoon into soup bowls. Top each with a spoonful of soured cream and then a spoonful of lumpfish roe. Serve immediately.

# Creamed Pear and Leek Refresher*

This is a delicately flavoured cold soup. For the less adventurous, use potatoes instead of pears!

**1**

Thinly pare the rind off half the lemon and cut into thin strips. Plunge into boiling water for 2 minutes, then drain, rinse with cold water and drain again. Reserve for garnish. Finely grate the remaining rind and squeeze the juice.

**2**

Fry (sauté) the leek and potato in the butter for 2 minutes, stirring, until softened but not browned.

**3**

Stir in the stock, vermouth, chopped pears and grated lemon rind. Bring to the boil, reduce the heat and simmer for 20 minutes until the vegetables are tender.

**4**

Purée in a blender or food processor, then turn into a bowl, season with salt, pepper and the mace and leave until cold.

**5**

Stir in the creams and spike with a little of the lemon juice. Chill.

**6**

To serve, pour into soup bowls and garnish each with a little of the reserved lemon rind and a tiny sprig of fresh parsley.

| SERVES 6 |
| --- |
| 1 lemon |
| 2 leeks, sliced |
| 1 large potato, diced |
| 15 g/½ oz/1 tbsp butter |
| 600 ml/1 pt/2½ cups vegetable stock |
| 45 ml/3 tbsp sweet white vermouth |
| 3 ripe pears, chopped |
| Salt and freshly ground black pepper |
| Pinch of ground mace |
| 300 ml/½ pt/1¼ cups single (light) cream |
| 150 ml/¼ pt/⅔ cup crème fraîche |
| TO GARNISH: |
| Tiny sprigs of parsley |

# Summer Salmon Bisque ✳

You can cheat and use canned salmon, but do make sure you have removed all the skin and bones before adding it.

### SERVES 6

1 small red (bell) pepper

1 onion, chopped

1 garlic clove, crushed

1 potato, finely diced

15 g/½ oz/1 tbsp butter or margarine

2 tomatoes, skinned and chopped

300 ml/½ pt/1¼ cups fish or chicken stock

225 g/8 oz salmon tail, skinned

1.5 ml/¼ tsp cayenne

5 ml/1 tsp dried dill (dill weed)

300 ml/½ pt/1¼ cups milk

30 ml/2 tbsp brandy

150 ml/¼ pt/⅔ cup double (heavy) cream

Salt and freshly ground black pepper

TO GARNISH:

Tiny sprigs of watercress

**1**

Cut six thin rings off the pepper. Plunge into boiling water for 1 minute, drain, rinse with cold water, drain and dry on kitchen paper (paper towels). Reserve for garnish.

**2**

Chop the remaining pepper, discarding the seeds and stalk. Place in a pan with the onion, garlic, potato and butter or margarine. Fry (sauté), stirring, for 2 minutes until softened but not browned.

**3**

Add the tomatoes and stock, bring to the boil, reduce the heat and simmer for 10 minutes until the vegetables are soft.

**4**

Add the salmon, cayenne and dill and simmer for 5 minutes or until the fish is tender. Stir in a little of the milk to cool the soup slightly.

**5**

Turn into a blender or food processor and purée until smooth. Pour into a bowl, stir in the remaining milk and leave until cold. Then stir in the brandy, cream and seasoning to taste. Chill well.

**6**

When ready to serve, pour into soup bowls. Float a reserved pepper ring on top and garnish each with a tiny sprig of watercress.

# Gazpacho with Prawns ✳

For vegetarians, hang slices of cucumber over the rim of the dishes instead of prawns.

## 1

Soak the bread in the water for 2 minutes. Place in a blender or food processor with the remaining ingredients except the seasoning, prawns and lemon.

## 2

Purée until smooth. Season to taste and chill.

## 3

To serve, pour into deep soup cups and hang three prawns over the rim of each. Add a slice of lemon and serve.

| SERVES 6 |
| --- |
| 2 slices of white bread, crusts removed |
| 150 ml/¼ pt/⅔ cup cold water |
| 30 ml/2 tbsp olive oil |
| 15 ml/1 tbsp white wine vinegar |
| 1 garlic clove, crushed |
| 2 × 400 g/14 oz/large cans of tomatoes |
| 30 ml/2 tbsp tomato purée (paste) |
| 1 red (bell) pepper, chopped |
| 5 cm/2 in piece of cucumber, roughly chopped |
| Salt and freshly ground black pepper |
| 18 unpeeled cooked prawns (shrimp) |
| 6 lemon slices |

# Memorable Main Courses

## Fragrant Herb Poussins with Lemon and Honey

You can use chicken portions instead of poussins, if necessary. See photograph on page 26.

### SERVES 6

6 poussins (Cornish hens)

6 sprigs each of parsley, thyme, sage and rosemary

45 ml/3 tbsp clear honey

30 ml/2 tbsp lemon juice

25 g/1 oz/2 tbsp butter

Salt and freshly ground black pepper

TO GARNISH:

Lemon twists

Sprigs of parsley

TO SERVE:

Wild Rice Salad (see page 94)

Mangetout (snow peas), blanched and tossed in French dressing

**1**

Wipe the poussins inside and out with kitchen paper (paper towels). Push a sprig of each herb into each bird. Place breast-sides down in a large roasting tin (pan).

**2**

Warm the honey, lemon and butter together with a little salt and pepper. Brush over the birds.

**3**

Roast in a preheated oven at 200°C/400°F/gas mark 6 for 25 minutes. Turn over, brush with the remaining honey mixture and continue roasting for a further 30–40 minutes until golden brown and the juices run clear when pierced at the thigh. Leave to cool, then pack in an airtight container and chill.

**4**

Serve garnished with lemon twists and sprigs of parsley with Wild Rice Salad and dressed mangetout.

# Peppered Beef Fillet with Horseradish Mayonnaise

Try this with thick pork tenderloin instead of beef and flavour the mayonnaise with grainy mustard instead of horseradish.

### 1
Trim the meat if necessary. Rub all over with the olive oil, then roll in the crushed peppercorns to coat completely.

### 2
Place in a roasting tin (pan).

### 3
Roast in a preheated oven at 220°C/425°F/gas mark 7 for 30 minutes for pink meat, 45 minutes for well done. Remove from the oven and leave to cool. Wrap in foil. Chill.

### 4
Mix the mayonnaise with the horseradish and fold in the whipped cream. Season to taste, stir in the parsley and pack in a small container.

### 5
To serve, carve the meat into 12 slices. Arrange two on each plate with a spoonful of the horseradish mayonnaise and a garnish of lollo rosso leaves. Serve with new potatoes and a celeriac and carrot salad.

| SERVES 6 |
| --- |
| 1 kg/2¼ lb piece of beef fillet |
| 30 ml/2 tbsp olive oil |
| 45 ml/3 tbsp pink, green and black peppercorns, coarsely crushed |
| 150 ml/¼ pt/⅔ cup mayonnaise |
| 30 ml/2 tbsp grated horseradish |
| 150 ml/¼ pt/⅔ cup whipping cream, whipped |
| Salt and freshly ground black pepper |
| 30 ml/2 tbsp chopped parsley |
| TO GARNISH: |
| Lollo rosso leaves |
| TO SERVE: |
| Hot new potatoes (see page 8) |
| Grated celeriac (celery root) and carrot, tossed in French dressing |

# Herb and Redcurrant Stuffed Duck ✳

If you give your butcher notice, he will bone the birds for you – but do try it yourself, it's not as difficult as it sounds!

### SERVES 8

1.75 kg/4 lb oven-ready duck

1.25 kg/2¾ lb oven-ready chicken

STUFFING:

100 g/4 oz/2 cups fresh breadcrumbs

Grated rind and juice of 1 orange

45 ml/3 tbsp redcurrant jelly (clear conserve)

15 ml/1 tbsp chopped thyme

15 ml/1 tbsp chopped parsley

100 g/4 oz/1 cup pine nuts

1 egg, beaten

Salt and freshly ground black pepper

2 large carrots, coarsely grated

15 ml/1 tbsp olive oil

TO GARNISH:

Orange slices

Sprigs of thyme

TO SERVE:

Potato Salad Speciality (see page 97)

Chicory (Belgian endive), watercress and fresh, stoned (pitted) cherries, dressed with French dressing

**1**

Bone the duck. Put it on a board with the neck towards you and cut off the wing and leg tips at the joint. Place breast-side down. Using a sharp knife, slit through to the bone along its back. Ease the flesh away from one side of the back and rib cage, then turn the bird round and repeat on the other side. Continue easing and scraping the flesh away until you meet the leg and wing joints. Cut through each joint at the socket. Continue to scrape the flesh away. Remove the wishbone and then carefully cut all the flesh from the breast bone, taking care not to cut through the skin. Cut off the parson's nose. Lift away the entire carcass (which you can use for stock).

**2**

Scrape the meat from the legs and wings, pushing back with a knife as you go. Cut the bones free when you reach the ends and tuck any loose flesh inside.

**3**

Repeat with the chicken.

**4**

Mix together the stuffing ingredients except the carrots and the olive oil. Season well.

**5**

Lay the duck skin-side down on a board. Carefully remove the skin from the chicken. Lay the chicken on top of the duck with the leg meat at opposite ends from the duck leg meat. Season. Spread half the stuffing down the length of the chicken. Cover with grated carrot. Top with the remaining stuffing. Wrap the duck up over the stuffing, tucking in the ends and overlapping along its back to form a neat parcel. Sew up with a trussing needle and string. Weigh and calculate the cooking time, allowing 25 minutes per 450 g/1 lb.

**6**

Place in a roasting tin (pan). Brush with olive oil and sprinkle with salt. Roast in a preheated oven at 190°C/375°F/gas mark 5 for the calculated cooking time.

**7**

Remove from the tin and leave to cool. Remove the string and wrap in foil.

**8**

Cut into slices and garnish with orange slices and sprigs of thyme. Serve with Potato Salad Speciality and a chicory, watercress and cherry salad.

### BONED POULTRY

**Any kind of poultry can be boned and stuffed, following the same instructions. Poussins, pheasant and other more unusual birds are now readily available in supermarkets. The advantage of boning the bird is that it looks great and is simplicity itself to carve, serve and eat.**

# Turkey and Cranberry Layered Pâté ✳

You can substitute chicken breasts for the turkey, or use corn relish instead of cranberry sauce.

| SERVES 6-8 |
| --- |
| 100 g/4 oz/½ cup butter |
| 450 g/1 lb turkey or chicken livers, chopped |
| 100 g/4 oz streaky bacon, rinded and diced |
| 1 garlic clove, crushed |
| 5 ml/1 tsp juniper berries, crushed |
| 15 ml/1 tbsp port |
| Salt and freshly ground black pepper |
| 100 g/4 oz/2 cups fresh breadcrumbs |
| 30 ml/2 tbsp chopped parsley |
| 15 ml/1 tbsp chopped sage |
| 1 small onion, finely chopped |
| 2 eggs, beaten |
| 2 turkey breast fillets, cut into neat pieces |
| 185 g/6½ oz/1 small jar of cranberry sauce |
| TO SERVE: |
| Colourful mixed pickles |
| Green salad |
| Focaccia with olives or sun-dried tomatoes |

1

Line a 900 g/2 lb loaf tin (pan) with non-stick baking parchment. Melt the butter in a saucepan. Add the livers, bacon, garlic and juniper berries and fry (sauté), stirring, for 2 minutes. Purée in a blender or food processor with the port and season well.

2

Mix the breadcrumbs with the herbs, onion and a little salt and pepper. Mix with the beaten eggs to bind.

3

Place half the turkey liver mixture in the base of the tin. Top with half the turkey meat, then half the stuffing. Add a layer of all the cranberry sauce, then a layer of the remaining stuffing, then the remaining turkey meat and finish with the remaining liver mixture.

4

Wrap the tin in foil and stand it in a roasting tin containing 2.5 cm/1 in boiling water. Bake in a preheated oven at 180°C/350°F/gas mark 4 for 1½ hours until just set and shrinking from the sides of the tin (don't worry if it looks pink and moist).

5

Remove from the oven, cover with clean foil and two saucers. Weigh down, leave until cold, then chill.

6

Serve sliced with colourful mixed pickles, a green salad and focaccia with olives or sun-dried tomatoes.

*Opposite: Summer Paella (page 60)*

# Seafood Millefeuille

You can use all prawns (shrimp) or chopped crabsticks instead of the seafood cocktail.

**1**

Unroll the thawed pastry and cut into three oblongs. Place on a dampened baking (cookie) sheet. Bake in a preheated oven at 220°C/425°F/gas mark 7 for 10–15 minutes until risen and golden. Cool, then carefully split each piece of pastry in half.

**2**

Drain the seafood cocktail on kitchen paper (paper towels). Mix with all but 30 ml/2 tbsp of the mayonnaise, the spring onions, seasoning and lemon juice.

**3**

Mash the cheese with the remaining mayonnaise and the tomato purée. Stir in the pimientos.

**4**

Place one sheet of pastry on the upturned lid of an airtight container. Spread a third of the seafood filling over. Spread a second piece of pastry with a third of the tomato mixture and place on top. Repeat with the remaining sheets of pastry and fillings so you finish with a layer of tomato mixture.

**5**

Lay the prawns down the centre and arrange the olives down either side. Finish with chopped parsley along both outside edges. Cover with the container base, pressing into position, and chill until ready to pack.

**6**

Serve with the prepared salads.

*Opposite: Raspberry Angel's Food Cake (page 67)*

| SERVES 6 |
| --- |
| 375 g/13 oz packet of frozen ready-rolled puff pastry (paste), thawed |
| FILLING: |
| 350 g/12 oz packet of frozen seafood cocktail, thawed |
| 150 ml/¼ pt/⅔ cup mayonnaise |
| 2 spring onions (scallions), finely chopped |
| Salt and freshly ground black pepper |
| Lemon juice to taste |
| 200 g/7 oz/scant 1 cup medium-fat soft cheese |
| 30 ml/2 tbsp tomato purée (paste) |
| 200 g/7 oz/1 small can of pimiento caps, drained and chopped |
| 6 unpeeled cooked prawns (shrimp) |
| 6 stoned (pitted) olives, halved |
| 30 ml/2 tbsp finely chopped parsley |
| TO SERVE: |
| Mixed green salad |
| Thinly sliced, peeled cucumber, dressed with cider vinegar and black pepper |

# Marinated Lamb and Spring Vegetables in Aspic

This is based on a traditional French dish using beef topside. It does take a little time but looks superb – and tastes great.

| SERVES 6 |
| --- |
| 1.5 kg/3 lb boned leg of lamb |
| MARINADE: |
| 2 onions, sliced |
| 2 carrots, sliced |
| 2 celery sticks, sliced |
| 1 garlic clove, crushed |
| 2 large sprigs of rosemary |
| Pinch of ground cloves |
| Salt and freshly ground black pepper |
| 600 ml/1 pt/2½ cups medium dry rosé wine |
| 15 ml/1 tbsp olive oil |
| 450 ml/¾ pt/2 cups lamb or chicken stock |
| 15 g/½ oz/1 tbsp powdered gelatine |
| 5 ml/1 tsp caster (superfine) sugar |
| SPRING VEGETABLES: |
| 225 g/8 oz baby carrots, scrubbed |
| 225 g/8 oz baby sweetcorn (corn) cobs |
| 225 g/8 oz small French (green) beans, topped, tailed and halved |
| 100 g/4 oz button mushrooms |
| TO GARNISH: |
| Small sprigs of rosemary (preferably in flower) |

1
Put the lamb in a bowl. Add all the marinade ingredients except the oil, stock, gelatine and sugar. Cover and leave to marinate for 24 hours, turning occasionally.

2
Drain the lamb and dry on kitchen paper (paper towels). Heat the oil in a flameproof casserole (Dutch oven) and fry (sauté) the meat on all sides to brown. Remove from the pan. Strain the marinade, reserving the liquid. Add the marinade vegetables to the pan and fry, stirring, for 2 minutes.

3
Return the meat to the pan. Pour the marinade over (including the rosemary) and add the stock and sugar. Bring to the boil, reduce the heat, part-cover and simmer over a very gentle heat for 2½ hours or until very tender. Do not boil fast. Leave to cool in the liquid. Remove the meat, wrap in foil and chill.

4
Skim off any fat from the surface of the cooking liquid, then strain into a clean pan. Sprinkle the gelatine over and leave to soften for 5 minutes. Heat gently, stirring until the gelatine has completely dissolved.

**5**

Meanwhile, steam the prepared spring vegetables or cook in a little boiling, lightly salted water until tender. They must be soft or they will harden when in the jelly. Drain, rinse with cold water and drain again.

**6**

Pour a thin layer of the gelatine stock in the base of a lightly oiled 1.5 kg/3 lb loaf tin (pan) or terrine. Arrange a layer of vegetables lengthways in it and chill until set.

**7**

Carve the meat into slices, discarding the string, and arrange down the centre on top of the set vegetables. Arrange some more vegetables down the sides. Pour enough of the gelatine stock over to cover and chill again to set.

**8**

Heat the remaining stock, if necessary, to melt. Arrange the remaining vegetables over the top and pour over the remaining gelatine stock. Chill until firm.

**TO SERVE:**

**Hot new potatoes (see page 8)**

**Green salad**

---

### STUNNING DISPLAY

**It is worth spending a little time and thought when you are creating a dish in aspic, as the presentation is so important. Cut the vegetables neatly and arrange them attractively as you layer the dish.**

# Vegetarian Sophisticate

Substitute French (green) beans for the asparagus, if you prefer.

### SERVES 8

175 g/6 oz baby carrots, scraped

100 g/4 oz baby asparagus spears

30 ml/2 tbsp powdered gelatine or
agar agar

100 ml/3½ fl oz/6½ tbsp dry white wine

40 g/1½ oz/3 tbsp butter or margarine

250 ml/8 fl oz/1 cup milk

Salt and freshly ground black pepper

1.5 ml/¼ tsp ground mace

100 g/4 oz/1 cup plain (all-purpose)
flour

2 eggs, separated

750 g/1½ lb/3 cups soft cheese

150 ml/¼ pt/⅔ cup double (heavy)
cream

30 ml/2 tbsp lemon or lime juice

TO GARNISH:

A few chive stalks

A few juniper berries

TO SERVE:

Hot new potatoes (see page 8)

Tomato and watercress salad with
French dressing

**1**

Boil the carrots for 10 minutes in lightly salted water and steam the asparagus in a steamer or colander over the pan for 4–5 minutes until just tender. Drain the carrots, rinse with cold water and leave both vegetables to cool.

**2**

Dissolve the gelatine or agar agar in the wine according to the packet directions.

**3**

Melt the butter or margarine in a saucepan. Add the milk, a little salt and pepper and the mace, then whisk in the flour until smooth. Bring to the boil and cook for 2 minutes, whisking all the time until thick.

**4**

Remove from the heat and whisk in the egg yolks. Then work in the cheese until well blended. Stir in half the dissolved gelatine or agar agar.

**5**

Whisk the egg whites until stiff, then whip the cream with the lemon or lime juice until softly peaking. Fold in the cream, then the egg whites into the cheese mixture. Taste and add more seasoning, if necessary.

**6**

Spoon about a third of the mixture into a 1.5 litre/
2½ pt/6 cup terrine. Top with the carrots in a single
layer. Add a further third of the cheese mixture, then
the asparagus spears, lain in alternate directions. Top
with the remaining cheese mixture and gently level the
surface. Chill until set.

**7**

Melt the remaining gelatine or agar agar. Pour over the
cheese. Lay a few chive stalks and juniper berries in
the gelatine to garnish and chill again until set. Wrap
in foil to transport and serve cut into slices with hot
new potatoes and a tomato and watercress salad.

### VEGETARIAN GUESTS

**Non-vegetarian and vegetarian
guests alike will enjoy this kind of
dish and you can't go wrong in your
planning if you include at least one
vegetarian recipe in your meal.
Remember not to use gelatine for a
strictly vegetarian version.**

# Spinach, Ricotta and Pecan Roulade with Sun-dried Tomato Dressing ✳

This is also delicious with cashew nuts instead of pecans.

## SERVES 6–8

ROULADES:

450 g/1 lb spinach, trimmed

5 ml/1 tsp grated nutmeg

90 ml/6 tbsp grated Parmesan cheese

Salt and freshly ground black pepper

8 eggs, separated

FILLING:

450 g/1 lb/2 cups Ricotta cheese

175 g/6 oz/1½ cups pecans, chopped

30 ml/2 tbsp snipped chives

DRESSING:

285 g/9½ oz/1 jar of sun-dried tomatoes in olive oil

Grated rind and juice of 1 small lemon

5 ml/1 tsp caster (superfine) sugar

½ small red chilli, seeded and chopped

TO SERVE:

Tabbouleh (see page 95)

Granary rolls

**1**

Lightly grease two 18 × 28 cm/7 × 11 in Swiss roll tins (jelly roll pans) and line with non-stick baking parchment standing 2.5 cm/1 in above the rim.

**2**

Thoroughly wash the spinach and shake off the excess water. Place in a saucepan with no extra water, cover and cook for 5 minutes or until tender. Drain off any water and chop.

**3**

Turn into a bowl, add the nutmeg, 60 ml/4 tbsp of the Parmesan cheese and a little salt and pepper. Beat in the egg yolks.

**4**

Whisk the egg whites until stiff and fold into the mixture with a metal spoon. Turn into the prepared tins and level the surfaces.

**5**

Bake in a preheated oven (side by side, if possible) at 200°C/400°F/gas mark 6 for 10–15 minutes until golden brown and firm to the touch.

**6**

Dust two sheets of baking parchment with the remaining Parmesan cheese. Turn out the roulades on to the paper, loosen the cooking paper with a round-bladed knife and leave on top. Cover with clean tea towels (dish cloths) and leave until cold.

**7**

Meanwhile, make the filling and dressing. Put the Ricotta in a bowl and beat in the pecans, chives and a little salt and pepper.

**8**

Put the contents of the jar of sun-dried tomatoes in a blender or food processor and purée. Add the lemon rind and juice, sugar, chilli and a little salt and pepper and run the machine again. Taste and re-season to taste. Thin with a little water, if necessary. Return to the jar for transporting.

**9**

When the roulades are cold, discard the cooking paper and trim the edges. Spread the Ricotta mixture over and roll up, using the paper underneath to help. Wrap in the paper for transporting.

**10**

To serve, cut into slices, arrange on plates with a spoonful of dressing on one side and serve with tabbouleh and granary rolls.

### NEW INGREDIENTS

Italian Ricotta cheese is now readily available in supermarkets, along with exciting ingredients from all over the world which used to be available only from the best city delicatessens. Don't be afraid to experiment with new foods as they become available.

# Summer Paella

Chilled paella is a masterpiece. It allows all the flavours to develop thoroughly. See photograph on page 51.

| SERVES 6 |
| --- |
| 450 g/1 lb mussels in their shells |
| 1.2 litres/2 pts/5 cups chicken stock |
| 1.25 kg/2¾ lb chicken, jointed into 6 pieces |
| Salt and freshly ground black pepper |
| 90 ml/6 tbsp olive oil |
| 1 Spanish onion, finely chopped |
| 1 garlic clove, crushed |
| 4 baby squid, cleaned and sliced into rings |
| 450 g/1 lb/2 cups risotto rice |
| 15 ml/1 tbsp paprika |
| 5 ml/1 tsp saffron powder |
| 1 bay leaf |
| 1 red (bell) pepper, sliced |
| 1 green pepper, sliced |
| 4 tomatoes, skinned and chopped |
| 100 g/4 oz frozen or shelled fresh peas |
| 12 unpeeled prawns (shrimp) |
| 6 black olives |
| TO GARNISH: |
| Lemon wedges |
| Chopped parsley |
| TO SERVE: |
| Focaccia |
| Green salad |

**1**

Scrub the mussels, discarding any that are damaged or won't close when sharply tapped. Remove the beards. Place in a saucepan with half the stock. Bring to the boil, cover and cook for a few minutes, shaking the pan occasionally until the mussels have opened. Leave to cool.

**2**

Wipe the chicken and season with a little salt and pepper. Heat the oil in a large paella pan or frying pan (skillet). Fry (sauté) the chicken on all sides to brown. Reduce the heat and cook for a further 10 minutes. Remove from the pan.

**3**

Add the onion and garlic and fry for 2 minutes until slightly softened. Add the squid and cook for 1 minute. Stir in the rice and cook, stirring, for 1 minute until coated with oil.

**4**

Strain the mussel liquor into the pan and add the remaining stock. Stir in the paprika, saffron and bay leaf. Return the chicken to the pan. Bring to the boil, cover with a lid or foil, reduce the heat and simmer gently for 15 minutes.

**5**

Add the peppers, tomatoes and peas and cook for a further 10 minutes until the rice has absorbed nearly all the liquid and is just tender, and the chicken is cooked through. Season to taste and stir gently. Remove from the heat. Leave to cool and then turn into a large airtight container.

**6**

Add the mussels still in their shells (or break off the top shells, if liked). Add the prawns and olives. Cover and chill until ready to transport. Wash the paella pan, if used, and take with you or pack a large shallow serving dish.

**7**

To serve, take the prawns and olives off the top. Turn the mixture into the paella pan or serving dish, making sure that some of the mussels are sitting on the top. Arrange the prawns and olives around. Garnish with lemon wedges and sprinkle with parsley. Serve with focaccia and a green salad.

### SUPERB SEAFOOD

**Seafood makes wonderful summer dishes, but always make sure that it is absolutely fresh, carefully prepared, and stored and transported to keep it cool and fresh until you are ready to eat.**

# Lobster Frigador

This is a chilled version of the famous Lobster Thermidor.

| SERVES 6 |
| --- |

3 small cooked lobsters

45 ml/3 tbsp olive oil

1 bunch of spring onions (scallions), chopped

120 ml/4 fl oz/½ cup mayonnaise

120 ml/4 fl oz/½ cup crème fraîche

30 ml/2 tbsp brandy

50 g/2 oz/½ cup strong Cheddar cheese, grated

Salt and freshly ground black pepper

1.5 ml/¼ tsp cayenne

25 g/1 oz/¼ cup Parmesan cheese, grated

Paprika

TO GARNISH:

Sprigs of parsley

Lemon wedges

TO SERVE:

Olive ciabatta

Mixed leaf salad

Sliced avocado, tossed in French dressing

**1**

Twist off and crack the lobster claws. Remove the meat. Cut each lobster in half lengthways along the back with a sharp knife and remove the stomach sacs, gills and the black vein running down the tails. Carefully remove the green, creamy livers in the heads and place in a fairly large bowl. Scoop out any coral in the tails and add to the bowl. Remove the meat and cut into neat pieces.

**2**

Wash and dry the shells.

**3**

Heat the oil in a frying pan (skillet) and fry (sauté) the spring onions for 1 minute to soften slightly. Remove from the heat and add to the liver and coral. Add the remaining ingredients, except the lobster meat, Parmesan cheese and paprika, seasoning to taste with the salt, pepper and cayenne. Mix well.

**4**

Fold in the lobster meat and pile back into the shells. Sprinkle with the Parmesan cheese and a little paprika and pack in an airtight container. Chill until ready to transport.

**5**

Garnish with sprigs of parsley and lemon wedges and serve with olive ciabatta, a mixed leaf salad and avocado slices, tossed in French dressing.

# Tantalising Desserts

## Iced Gin and Lemon Sorbets ❄

Try using vodka and lime for an equally stunning creation.

### 1

Cut the tops off the lemons and carefully scoop out the flesh. Cut a small slice off the base of each so they stand up, taking care not to make a hole in the base. Place in the freezer.

### 2

Purée the flesh in a blender or food processor, then strain into a bowl.

### 3

Heat the sugar, water and glucose in a saucepan until the sugar has dissolved. Bring to the boil and boil for 1 minute. Leave to cool.

### 4

Stir into the strained lemon juice and add the gin. Pour into a shallow container and freeze for 2 hours until hardening around the edges. Whisk until all the ice crystals have broken up. Return to the freezer. Whisk again after 1 hour, then freeze until just firm. Pack into the lemons and return to the freezer. Transport in a cool box surrounded with ice packs.

### 5

To serve, stand on individual plates or in glass dishes and decorate with tiny sprigs of mint.

### SERVES 6

6 lemons

350 g/12 oz/1½ cups caster (superfine) sugar

250 ml/8 fl oz/1 cup water

30 ml/2 tbsp liquid glucose

250 ml/8 fl oz/1 cup gin

TO DECORATE:

Tiny sprigs of mint

# Tropical Fruit Salads with Mango Coulis

If you can't buy small pineapples, use one large one and serve in dishes instead of the pineapple shells.

### SERVES 6

3 small pineapples

1 passion fruit

1 pawpaw

1 banana

Lime or lemon juice

100 g/4 oz seedless (pitless) black grapes

MANGO COULIS:

2 ripe mangoes

60 ml/4 tbsp caster (superfine) sugar

30 ml/2 tbsp rum

**1**

Cut each pineapple in half lengthways, leaving the green tops on. Using a serrated-edged knife, cut out the flesh, leaving a thin border all round.

**2**

Discard any woody central core, cut the flesh into small neat pieces and place in a bowl with a lid.

**3**

Halve the passion fruit and scoop the seeds into the bowl.

**4**

Peel and dice the pawpaw, discarding the black seeds, and add to the bowl.

**5**

Cut the banana into 1 cm/½ in chunks and toss in a little lime or lemon juice. Add to the bowl with the grapes. Toss gently and cover with the lid. Chill until ready to pack. Pack the pineapple shells separately.

**6**

Peel and cut all the mango flesh off the stones (pits) into a blender or food processor. Add the sugar and rum. Run the machine until smooth. Add lime or lemon juice to taste. Pour into a small container with a lid.

**7**

To serve, pile the fruits back into the pineapple shells. Place on serving plates. Pour the mango coulis into six dishes. Using a fork, guests spear a piece of the fruit and dip in the coulis before eating.

# Chocolate Marble Cheesecakes *

Plain vanilla cheesecakes are delicious too. Simply omit the chocolate and decorate with soured (dairy sour) cream.

## 1
Line six ramekin dishes (custard cups) with greased foil, so that it stands about 4 cm/1½ in above the rims of the dishes. Mix the crushed biscuits with two-thirds of the butter and press into the bases of the dishes.

## 2
Beat the sugar and vanilla into the cheese. Melt the chocolate in a bowl over a pan of hot water (or in the microwave). Beat in the remaining melted butter. Fold into the cheese to give a marbled effect.

## 3
Spoon over the biscuit bases and level the surfaces. Chill until firm.

## 4
Holding the block of chocolate on its side in one hand, use a potato peeler to scrape curls of chocolate off the side of the block. Arrange the chocolate curls on top of the cheesecakes to decorate. Chill until ready to transport, still in the ramekins.

## 5
To serve, lift out of the dishes, using the foil. Peel off the foil and place on individual plates. Serve with pouring cream, if liked.

### SERVES 6

200 g/7 oz/1 small packet of chocolate digestive biscuits (graham crackers), crushed

75 g/3 oz/⅓ cup unsalted (sweet) butter, melted

45 ml/3 tbsp icing (confectioners') sugar, sifted

5 ml/1 tsp vanilla essence (extract)

450 g/1 lb/2 cups Mascarpone cheese

100 g/4 oz plain (semi-sweet) chocolate, broken into pieces

TO DECORATE:

1 small block of plain chocolate

TO SERVE:

Pouring cream (optional)

# Chocolate Mocha Cups ✳

Try using white chocolate for the cups and white chocolate spread for the filling, but if you do this omit the coffee.

| SERVES 6 |
| --- |

**24 squares plain (semi-sweet) chocolate**

or

**6 ready-made chocolate cases (available in most good supermarkets)**

FILLING:

**150 ml/¼ pt/⅔ cup double (heavy) cream**

**30 ml/2 tbsp dark chocolate spread**

**10 ml/2 tsp instant coffee powder**

**15 ml/1 tbsp brandy**

TO DECORATE:

**Chocolate coffee beans**

**6 silk or fresh flowers to match your colour scheme**

1

If making your own chocolate cases, melt the chocolate in a bowl over a pan of hot water (or in the microwave).

2

Put 15 ml/1 tbsp of chocolate into each of eight paper cases (make two extra cases to allow for breakages).

3

Press a second paper case into each, gently easing the chocolate up the sides between the cases. Do not press too hard and try to get an even coating.

4

Chill until firm, then gently peel off the paper cases. (The more you make these, the easier they get!)

5

Whip the cream until peaking, then blend in the chocolate spread. Dissolve the coffee in the brandy and stir in.

6

Spoon into the chocolate cups and swirl the tops with a spoon. Decorate each with chocolate coffee beans and place in an airtight container. Chill until ready to pack, surrounded by ice packs.

7

To serve, place a chocolate cup on each of six small serving plates and lay a flower to the side of each.

# Raspberry Angel's Food Cake *

Store the egg yolks in water in the fridge; they can be used to glaze pies and enrich pastry (paste). See photograph on page 52.

## 1

Dust a 1.2 litre/2 pt/5 cup plain or fluted ring tin (pan) with a little flour, shaking off any excess, but do not grease.

## 2

Whisk the egg whites until frothy, then whisk in the cream of tartar and continue to whisk until stiff.

## 3

Sift the sugar and flours together twice. Lightly fold into the egg whites a little at a time, using a metal spoon. Add the vanilla essence at the same time.

## 4

Turn into the floured tin and bake in a preheated oven at 160°C/325°F/gas mark 3 for 30 minutes. Leave to cool in the tin.

## 5

Turn out on to a serving plate that will fit in an airtight container. Fill the centre with crème fraîche and top with as many of the raspberries as you can. Arrange the remainder around the edge of the cake. Dust with a little icing sugar and chill until ready to pack.

| SERVES 6 |
| --- |
| Flour for dusting |
| 4 egg whites |
| 2.5 ml/½ tsp cream of tartar |
| 150 g/5 oz/⅔ cup caster (superfine) sugar |
| 40 g/1½ oz/⅓ cup plain (all-purpose) flour |
| 25 g/1 oz/¼ cup cornflour (cornstarch) |
| 5 ml/1 tsp vanilla essence (extract) |
| 150 ml/¼ pt/⅔ cup crème fraîche |
| 225 g/8 oz raspberries |
| A little icing (confectioners') sugar |

# Caribbean Eclairs ✳

Coffee-flavoured icing (frosting) makes an exciting alternative to the chocolate topping on these éclairs.

## SERVES 6

**CHOUX PASTRY (PASTE):**

65 g/2½ oz/scant ¾ cup plain (all-purpose) flour

Pinch of salt

25 g/1 oz/2 tbsp butter

150 ml/¼ pt/⅔ cup water

1 egg, beaten

**FILLING:**

1 large ripe banana

10 ml/2 tsp lemon juice

15 ml/1 tbsp caster (superfine) sugar

150 ml/¼ pt/⅔ cup double (heavy) cream

30 ml/2 tbsp rum

**TOPPING:**

100 g/4 oz/⅔ cup icing (confectioners') sugar

15 g/½ oz/2 tbsp cocoa (unsweetened chocolate) powder

Water

**1**

Sift the flour and salt on to a sheet of greaseproof (waxed) paper. Place next to the hob so it is ready to use later.

**2**

Heat the butter and water in a saucepan until the fat melts, then bring to the boil. Add the flour all at once and beat with a wooden spoon until the mixture is smooth and leaves the sides of the pan clean.

**3**

Remove from the heat and beat for 30 seconds to cool slightly. Gradually beat in the egg, a little at a time, beating well after each addition until smooth and glossy but still holding its shape.

**4**

Spoon or pipe the mixture into six sausage shapes, about 12.5 cm/5 in long, well apart on a greased baking (cookie) sheet.

**5**

Bake in a preheated oven at 200°C/400°F/gas mark 6 for about 15–18 minutes until risen, crisp and golden brown. Cool on a wire rack.

**6**

Make a slit in the side of each and pull out any uncooked dough.

**7**

Mash the banana with the lemon juice and sugar until smooth. Whip the cream and rum until peaking, then fold in the banana. Use to fill the éclairs.

**8**

Sift the icing sugar and cocoa into a bowl. Mix with a teaspoon of cold water at a time to form a smooth, spreadable paste. Spread over the éclairs and leave to set. Pack in an airtight container.

---

**CHOUX ECLAIRS**

Choux pastry is remarkably easy to make and very versatile as it perfectly offsets so many toppings and fillings. Don't assemble choux éclairs too soon before transporting, though, otherwise they may go soggy. You can freeze the éclairs before filling.

---

# Alpine Fresh Figs

There is no real substitute for fresh figs, but dates make a delicious alternative.

**1**

Mix the nuts with the sugar on a plate. Use to coat the goats' cheese slices completely. Place in an airtight container and chill.

**2**

When ready to serve, quarter the figs. Place a leaf on each of six individual plates. Place a piece of the coated cheese in the centre with the four wedges of fig around. Eat with dessert knives and forks.

---

**SERVES 6**

100 g/4 oz/1 cup pistachio nuts, chopped

30 ml/2 tbsp light brown sugar

1 cylindrical goats' cheese, cut into 6 slices

6 fresh ripe figs

6 fig or vine leaves

# Strawberry Pavlovas

Use any fresh fruits to top these melt-in-the-mouth meringue nests.

| SERVES 6 |
| --- |

**6 egg whites**

**275 g/10 oz/1¼ cups caster (superfine) sugar**

**7.5 ml/1½ tsp vanilla essence (extract)**

**7.5 ml/1½ tsp cornflour (cornstarch)**

**7.5 ml/1½ tsp white wine vinegar**

TO FILL AND DECORATE:

**300 ml/½ pt/1¼ cups double (heavy) cream**

**30 ml/2 tbsp strawberry or orange liqueur**

**450 g/1 lb small strawberries, hulled**

**Angelica 'leaves'**

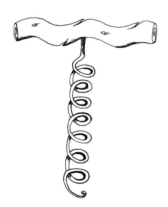

**1**

Mark six 7.5 cm/3 in circles well apart on a sheet of non-stick baking parchment on a baking (cookie) sheet.

**2**

Whisk the egg whites until stiff. Gradually whisk in the sugar until stiff and glossy.

**3**

Whisk in the vanilla essence, cornflour and vinegar.

**4**

Spoon on to the circles and spread to form 'nests', using the circles as a guide for size.

**5**

Bake in a preheated oven at 150°C/300°F/gas mark 2 for 1 hour. Turn off the heat and leave in the oven to cool. Peel off the paper gently, and store in an airtight container.

**6**

Whip the cream with the liqueur and chill. Just before you leave for the picnic, spoon the cream into the pavlovas and top with strawberries, all pointing upwards. Decorate with angelica 'leaves' and transport in the airtight container.

# Almond Crème Brûlée

If you are fond of caramelised sugar, treat yourself to a cook's blow torch to melt and brown the surface.

### SERVES 6

6 amaretti biscuits (cookies), crushed

30 ml/2 tbsp amaretto or kirsch

4 egg yolks

75 ml/5 tbsp caster (superfine) sugar

300 ml/½ pt/1¼ cups milk

300 ml/½ pt/1¼ cups double (heavy) cream

5 ml/1 tsp almond essence (extract)

50 g/2 oz/½ cup flaked (slivered) almonds

**1**

Divide the crushed amaretti biscuits between six lightly greased ramekin dishes (custard cups). Drizzle the liqueur over.

**2**

Whisk the egg yolks and 30 ml/2 tbsp caster sugar together until thick and pale.

**3**

Warm the milk, cream and almond essence together. Whisk into the egg yolk mixture. Stand the bowl over a pan of hot water and stir over a moderate heat until the custard thickens. Do not allow it to boil or it will curdle.

**4**

Pour the mixture over the crushed biscuits and leave to cool, then chill.

**5**

Sprinkle the almonds over, then cover completely with caster sugar.

**6**

Place under a hot grill (broiler) until the sugar has caramelised. Leave to cool, then chill again until ready to pack.

# Mulled Claret Jelly with Frosted Currants

Use any full-bodied red wine for these simple-to-make but luxurious-tasting jellies.

### SERVES 6

75 g/3 oz/⅓ cup caster (superfine) sugar

120 ml/4 fl oz/½ cup water

1 small lemon, cut into slices

2 cinnamon sticks

3 cloves

20 ml/4 tsp powdered gelatine

1 bottle of claret

TO DECORATE:

6 sprigs of redcurrants

Extra caster (superfine) sugar

TO SERVE:

Whipped cream

**1**

Put the measured amount of caster sugar in a pan with the water, lemon slices and spices. Bring to the boil, reduce the heat and simmer for 5 minutes, stirring occasionally. Strain, then stir in the gelatine until dissolved.

**2**

Mix with the claret and pour into six individual dishes. Chill until set. Pack in a rigid container.

**3**

Meanwhile, dip the redcurrant sprigs in water, shake off the excess, then coat with caster sugar. Leave to dry. Pack separately.

**4**

When ready to serve, lay a sprig of currants on top of each jelly. Serve with whipped cream.

# Barbecues for Every Occasion

There is nothing quite so delicious as food cooked in the open air over charcoal, from simple steaks or burgers to succulent cuts of meat or fish or colourful vegetables, marinated in wine, fragrant herbs and spices and seared to perfection. Set the tastebuds tingling with a little appetiser; then serve your main course with exciting salads, side dishes and sauces; round off the meal with something sweet and sinful, either hot off the barbecue or icy from the freezer, and you know you've got a winning combination. But it's not just the food, it's the whole ambience of a barbecue party that makes it so special.

In this chapter you will find everything you need to know about getting a barbecue party organised, from the pre-planning right through to making sure you get to sit down and eat with your guests … and some fantastic recipes of course!

For quick grills that taste great barbecued, see Everyday Outdoor Eating (page 114).

# KNOW-HOW

All barbecues take a bit of planning, so follow these simple guidelines:

● Unless you have a gas barbecue, check you have enough briquettes of compressed charcoal (most people find them more reliable than lump charcoal), firelighters, tapers and matches. If using gas, check the level in the cylinder in advance.

● Line the barbecue with foil first for easier cleaning.

● Get the fire lit in plenty of time. It takes at least 25 minutes, often longer, to reach the white heat stage, ready for cooking. Remember, the coals will maintain their heat for some time, so it's better to get the fire hot early than be panicking because it's not ready. The heat is right when the coals look grey and powdery and you can hold your hand about 10 cm/4 in above them for only 2–3 seconds.

● Have a poker handy, to spread the coals once they are white hot, and long-handled barbecue tools for turning, basting, etc.

● Prepare food well in advance to allow time for any marinating. Follow recipes for individual salads to see if they should be dressed in advance or at the last minute. Don't dress a green salad until you are ready to eat it or the leaves will wilt.

● Don't take foodstuffs out to the barbecue until you are ready to cook/eat. They won't take kindly to being left in the sun.

● Have finger bowls and plenty of napkins to hand – barbecue eating can be a messy business.

● You'll need one table or a trolley for the food and another for sitting at.

● Choose sturdy crockery, cutlery and glassware. I find wooden platters are better than china dinner plates as they don't cool the food so quickly and are (almost) unbreakable.

● Put foods that take the longest to cook on the barbecue first. I like to have the main course cooked and wrapped in foil in a roasting tin on the edge of the barbecue to keep warm. Then cook the starters (if you're having any) so you can all sit down together. Alternatively serve dips or cocktail nibbles with pre-meal drinks while you are cooking the main course.

● Keep a spray bottle of water near the barbecue when cooking to douse any flames.

● Don't cook the food too near the coals or it will burn. Oil the barbecue rack and place it about 10 cm/4 in above the coals.

● Any barbecued desserts can be put on the barbecue while you are eating your main course – or let guests have a rest between courses while you cook the desserts – they never take long on the barbecue anyway. Alternatively, serve ice cream or sorbet with a hot sauce; simply make the sauce in advance and heat it at the side of the barbecue while you eat your main course.

# Top Tips

For a wonderful aroma, throw a few pine cones or sprigs of fresh herbs or a scattering of dried ones directly on the coals as you start cooking.

Have a roll of kitchen paper (paper towels) handy to mop up spills and for really messy eaters.

If you don't want to make your own, buy a selection of dips and serving sauces or relishes – a whole range is available in any supermarket.

Brush pricked jacket potatoes with oil and sprinkle with salt, then wrap in foil and boil or pressure-cook before putting them on the barbecue to 'finish off'. Alternatively, cook them in the microwave, then season and wrap in foil before transferring to the barbecue. If cooking from raw, wrap them and put them directly in the embers of the fire (they'll take about 45 minutes to cook).

Spare ribs and chicken portions on the bone often benefit from being part-cooked before barbecuing (it ensures tenderness for the ribs, and thorough cooking for chicken which should never be served pink).

Don't go mad. It's better to have one perfectly cooked starter, main course and pudding than masses of different things burned to a frazzle! But if you are planning to have a mixed grill – sausages, burgers, chops, steak and so on – you'll only need one piece of each item per person. It's an enormous quantity of meat for one meal!

# Drinks

Anything goes for a barbecue. Many people like to start off with a fruit punch, wine cup or Pimms, then go on to wine. Others prefer to offer chilled lagers or cider (see Hampers with Style, page 35). Remember always to include plenty of chilled soft drinks and water for those who prefer not to drink alcohol.

# Sizzling Starters

## Marinated Scallops with Cured Ham and Oranges

This is an exciting version of scallops wrapped in bacon.

| SERVES 6 |
| --- |
| 12 scallops, shelled |
| Grated rind and juice of 1 orange |
| 30 ml/2 tbsp olive oil |
| 15 ml/1 tbsp white wine vinegar |
| 5 ml/1 tsp dried mixed herbs |
| Freshly ground black pepper |
| 4 thin slices of Westphalian ham |
| 2 small oranges, each cut into 6 slices and halved |
| TO GARNISH: |
| 175 g/6 oz mixed salad leaves, tossed in a little olive oil, vinegar, salt and freshly ground black pepper |

**1**

Cut the scallops into quarters. Mix the orange rind and juice, olive oil, vinegar, herbs and some pepper in a shallow dish. Add the scallops, toss and leave to marinate for at least 1 hour.

**2**

Cut each slice of ham into six strips. Wrap one around each scallop quarter. Thread on to 12 soaked wooden skewers, interspersing with half slices of orange.

**3**

Barbecue for about 2 minutes on each side until lightly golden and the scallops are just cooked, brushing frequently with any remaining marinade during cooking.

**4**

Put the tossed salad leaves on six plates and top with the kebabs.

*Opposite: Roasted Mediterranean Vegetables (page 100)*

# Halloumi Cheese with Bacon

This is a Greek speciality, often served as part of a Metze meal.

**1**

Stretch the bacon rashers with the back of a knife. Wrap one around each piece of cheese. Secure with a cocktail stick (toothpick), if necessary.

**2**

Place in a shallow dish and drizzle with a little olive oil. Add a good grinding of black pepper.

**3**

Barbecue for 2–3 minutes on each side until the bacon is crisp and the cheese is golden.

**4**

Meanwhile, warm the pitta breads briefly on both sides on the barbecue. Cut in half widthways. Open up slightly to form pockets. Fill with shredded lettuce. Put one of the cheese and bacon parcels in each and serve garnished with quartered cherry tomatoes.

### SERVES 6

200 g/7 oz/1 block of Halloumi cheese, cut into 6 slices

6 rashers (slices) of streaky bacon, rinded

Olive oil

Freshly ground black pepper

3 pitta breads

Shredded lettuce

TO GARNISH:

12 cherry tomatoes, quartered

*Opposite: Honey-mulled Peaches or Nectarines (page 107)*

# Garlic Tiger-prawn Kebabs

Crispy garlic bread cases are the perfect vehicle for all kinds of kebabs – or even sausages!

### SERVES 6

3 finger rolls

100 g/4 oz/½ cup unsalted (sweet) butter

2 garlic cloves, crushed

Salt and freshly ground black pepper

24 raw tiger-prawns (jumbo shrimp), peeled, with the tails left on

TO GARNISH:

Chopped parsley

TO SERVE:

Lemon wedges

**1**

Cut the finger rolls in half lengthways. Pull out the soft bread centres to leave hollow 'shells'.

**2**

Melt the butter with the garlic and a little salt and pepper. Brush all over the bread rolls. Place on a baking (cookie) sheet and bake in a preheated oven at 190°C/375°F/gas mark 5 for about 12 minutes until turning golden. Wrap in a foil parcel and keep warm at the side of the barbecue.

**3**

Thread the tiger-prawns on six skewers. Place on foil on the barbecue and brush with the remaining garlic butter. Cook for about 2 minutes on each side until just cooked through. Brush with any remaining garlic butter during cooking.

**4**

Slide a skewer of prawns into each bread 'bed'. Drizzle with any juices on the foil and sprinkle with chopped parsley. Serve with lemon wedges.

# Sardines with Fresh Tomato Chilli Salsa

Small mackerel or herring are equally delicious in this recipe; serve one for each person.

**1**

*P*lace the sardines on a hinged wire cooking rack. Brush with oil and season with salt and pepper. Close, turn over, open the rack and oil and season the other sides. Close the rack again.

**2**

Put all the salsa ingredients in a bowl with a little salt and pepper and mix well. Leave to stand until ready to serve.

**3**

Place the fish in their rack on the barbecue and cook for about 3 minutes on each side until golden brown and cooked through. Serve with the salsa and lime wedges.

| SERVES 6 |
| --- |
| 12 sardines, cleaned |
| Olive oil |
| Salt and freshly ground black pepper |
| SALSA: |
| 6 tomatoes, skinned, seeded and finely chopped |
| ½ small onion, grated |
| 1 red chilli, seeded and finely chopped |
| 15 ml/1 tbsp chopped parsley |
| 15 ml/1 tbsp snipped chives |
| 5 ml/1 tsp clear honey |
| Grated rind and juice of 1 lime |
| TO SERVE: |
| Lime wedges |

# Indonesian Vegetable Kebabs

The peanut dip is equally good with chicken, beef or pork kebabs.

| SERVES 6 |
| --- |

1 sweetcorn (corn) cob, cut into
  6 chunks

1 large courgette (zucchini), cut into
  6 chunks

1 large under-ripe banana, peeled and
  cut into 6 chunks

6 small tomatoes

30 ml/2 tbsp olive oil

5 ml/1 tsp lemon juice

Salt and freshly ground black pepper

SPICY PEANUT DIP:

90 ml/6 tbsp white wine vinegar

30 ml/2 tbsp light brown sugar

90 ml/6 tbsp water

60 ml/4 tbsp smooth peanut butter

5 ml/1 tsp grated fresh root ginger

30 ml/2 tbsp light soy sauce

1.5 ml/¼ tsp chilli powder

10 ml/2 tsp chopped coriander
  (cilantro)

TO GARNISH:

Sprigs of coriander

**1**

Thread a piece of each vegetable and fruit on six soaked wooden skewers. Brush with half the oil and the lemon juice and season lightly.

**2**

Boil the vinegar, sugar and water for 2 minutes, stirring, until the sugar has dissolved. Beat in the remaining ingredients and add the remaining olive oil. Keep warm at the side of the barbecue.

**3**

Barbecue the vegetable kebabs for about 4 minutes on each side until golden and tender. Garnish with sprigs of coriander and serve with the warm peanut dip.

# Warm Red Mullet and Grapefruit Salad

When red mullet are not available, use small salmon tail fillets.

**1**

Over a bowl to catch any drips, using a serrated knife, cut off all the rind and pith from the grapefruit. Cut the fruit into segments between each membrane. Put the segments to one side and squeeze the membranes to extract the juice.

**2**

Dry-fry the bacon in a small saucepan (suitable for transferring to the barbecue) until crisp. Remove from the pan with a draining spoon.

**3**

Arrange the salad leaves, bacon, onion rings and grapefruit segments attractively on six serving plates. Place on a tray or trolley to take out to the barbecue when ready to cook.

**4**

Stir 45 ml/3 tbsp of the olive oil and the vinegar into the bacon fat in the pan. Add the grapefruit juice, sugar and a little salt and pepper. Heat through. Keep warm at the side of the barbecue (do not allow to boil).

**5**

Put the fish in a hinged wire cooking rack. Brush with the remaining oil and season lightly on both sides. Barbecue for 3–4 minutes on each side until cooked through.

**6**

Place a fillet on top of each plate of salad. Spoon a little of the warm dressing over and serve.

| SERVES 6 |
| --- |
| 2 pink grapefruit |
| 6 rashers (slices) of streaky bacon, diced |
| 225 g/8 oz mixed salad leaves, including lollo rosso |
| 1 red onion, thinly sliced |
| 60 ml/4 tbsp olive oil |
| 30 ml/2 tbsp red wine vinegar |
| 10 ml/2 tsp light brown sugar |
| Salt and freshly ground black pepper |
| 6 fillets of red mullet |

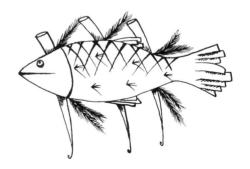

# Barbecued Garlic and Herb Mushrooms

Choose open 'cup' mushrooms which will hold the garlic butter.

| SERVES 6 |
| --- |
| 100 g/4 oz/½ cup unsalted (sweet) butter |
| 2 garlic cloves, crushed |
| 15 ml/1 tbsp chopped parsley |
| 15 ml/1 tbsp chopped thyme |
| Salt and freshly ground black pepper |
| 12 large open mushrooms, peeled and stalks trimmed |
| TO GARNISH: |
| A little freshly grated Parmesan cheese |
| TO SERVE: |
| French bread |

**1**
Mash the butter with the garlic, herbs and a little salt and pepper. Shape into a roll on a piece of greaseproof (waxed) paper and chill.

**2**
Place the mushrooms, gills up, on a large shallow tray. Cut the garlic butter into 12 slices and place a slice on each mushroom.

**3**
Oil the barbecue rack, lay the mushrooms on it, butter-side up and barbecue until the butter has melted and is sizzling. Dust with Parmesan cheese and serve straight away with lots of French bread.

# Citrus Corn Cobs

Add a little fire with a good pinch of chilli powder, if liked, instead of or as well as the cinnamon.

**1**

Mash the butter with the grated orange, lemon and lime rinds, the cinnamon and a little salt and pepper.

**2**

Lay the cobs on six pieces of foil, shiny side up, and spread all over with the butter mixture.

**3**

Wrap loosely but securely.

**4**

Barbecue for 12–15 minutes until the corn is tender, turning occasionally. Transfer to serving plates and allow guests to unwrap their own to get the full fragrance of the corn.

NOTE: If the cobs are large, which means they might not be so tender, par-boil in lightly salted water for 5 minutes and drain thoroughly before coating with the flavoured butter and wrapping in foil.

| SERVES 6 |
| --- |
| 100 g/4 oz/½ cup unsalted (sweet) butter |
| Grated rind of each of 1 orange, lemon and lime |
| 5 ml/1 tsp ground cinnamon |
| Salt and freshly ground black pepper |
| 6 sweetcorn (corn) cobs, husks removed |

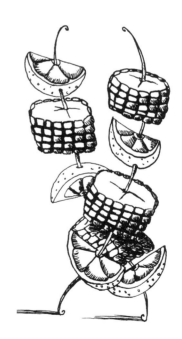

# Magnificent Main Courses

## Fijian Fish Steaks

These look stunning laid on a bed of washed vine leaves with the sauce to one side.

### SERVES 6

6 swordfish, tuna or shark steaks, skinned

400 g/14 oz/1 large can of coconut milk

45 ml/3 tbsp sunflower oil

2 garlic cloves, crushed

5 ml/1 tsp grated fresh root ginger

1 small green chilli, seeded and chopped

15 ml/1 tbsp chopped coriander (cilantro)

Grated rind and juice of 1 lime

TO GARNISH:

Lime wedges

Sprigs of coriander

TO SERVE:

Wild Rice Salad (see page 94)

**1**

Wipe the fish so that it is clean and dry, then place in a single layer in a large shallow dish, arranging so that they do not overlap.

**2**

Mix together 45 ml/3 tbsp of the coconut milk and the remaining ingredients and pour over the fish. Leave to marinate for at least 2 hours, turning once.

**3**

Drain off the marinade into a saucepan. Add the remaining coconut milk and bring to the boil. Boil rapidly until reduced by half, stirring occasionally. Season to taste. Keep warm at the side of the barbecue.

**4**

Barbecue the fish steaks for about 4–5 minutes on each side until cooked through, turning once. Spoon a little of the warm sauce on to serving plates. Top with the fish, garnish with lime wedges and sprigs of coriander and serve with Wild Rice Salad.

# South American Mackerel

You can use any oily fish for this recipe. It's not only delicious but very healthy too!

**1**

Slash the mackerel in several places on both sides. This will help the flavourings to penetrate the flesh.

**2**

Mix the onion, garlic, chilli, pimientos, passata and olives together and spoon on to the centres of six large squares of oiled foil, shiny sides up.

**3**

Lay a fish on top of each and season. Wrap loosely in the foil, twisting the edges together to seal securely.

**4**

Make the salsa. Scoop the avocado flesh into a bowl and mash with a little lemon juice. Add the grated onion, then gradually beat in the oil to form a smooth emulsion. Spike with more lemon juice and the Tabasco and Worcestershire sauces. Season to taste. Spoon into a bowl.

**5**

Barbecue the fish parcels for 20–25 minutes, turning once, until the fish is cooked through. Transfer the parcels to serving plates, open the foil and serve hot with the guacamole salsa, warm flour tortillas and a green salad.

**SERVES 6**

6 mackerel, cleaned

1 onion, thinly sliced

1 garlic clove, crushed

1 green chilli, seeded and chopped

400 g/14 oz/1 large can of pimientos, drained and sliced

30 ml/2 tbsp passata (sieved tomatoes)

12 stuffed green olives, sliced

Olive oil for greasing

Salt and freshly ground black pepper

GUACAMOLE SALSA:

2 ripe avocados, halved and stoned (pitted)

Lemon juice

5 ml/1 tsp grated onion

150 ml/¼ pt/⅔ cup olive oil

Tabasco sauce

Worcestershire sauce

TO SERVE:

Warm flour tortillas

Green salad

# Tandoori-style Chicken Breasts

Use chicken legs or thighs, if you prefer; allow at least two per person.

| SERVES 6 |
| --- |
| 6 chicken breasts, skinned |
| 150 ml/¼ pt/⅔ cup plain yoghurt |
| 2 garlic cloves, crushed |
| 15 ml/1 tbsp lemon juice |
| 1.5 ml/¼ tsp chilli powder |
| 5 ml/1 tsp ground cumin |
| 2.5 ml/½ tsp ground allspice |
| 30 ml/2 tbsp paprika |
| 5 ml/1 tsp ground coriander (cilantro) |
| 2.5 ml/½ tsp ground ginger |
| 10 ml/2 tsp garam masala |
| TO GARNISH: |
| Shredded lettuce |
| Lemon wedges |
| Onion rings |
| TO SERVE: |
| Wild Rice Salad (see page 94) |
| Finely diced cucumber in plain yoghurt, flavoured with chopped mint |

1
Make several slashes in the chicken breasts with a sharp knife, then lay them in a shallow dish.

2
Mix all the remaining ingredients together and spoon over the chicken. Leave to marinate for at least 4 hours, preferably overnight.

3
Drain from the marinade. Barbecue for 5–6 minutes on each side, turning occasionally until cooked through and slightly blackened in places. Brush with the marinade during cooking.

4
Serve garnished with shredded lettuce, lemon wedges and onion rings, with a Wild Rice Salad and cucumber in yoghurt with mint.

# Country Fruited Pork Olives

This is based on traditional beef olives, but is much quicker to cook. Use beef, if you prefer, but omit the apple in the stuffing.

**1**

Place a slice of pork in a plastic bag and beat with a rolling pin or meat mallet to flatten. Repeat with the remaining slices of meat.

**2**

Fry (sauté) half the chopped onion in the butter for 2 minutes, stirring, to soften. Stir in the remaining stuffing ingredients.

**3**

Spread over the slices of meat and roll up. Secure with wooden cocktail sticks (toothpicks).

**4**

Make the sauce. Heat half the oil in a saucepan (suitable for transferring to the barbecue). Add the remaining sauce ingredients and a little salt and pepper. Bring to the boil and simmer for about 8 minutes until pulpy, stirring occasionally.

**5**

Brush the pork olives with the remaining oil. Barbecue for 6–7 minutes on each side until cooked through and golden. Remove the cocktail sticks and serve with the tomato sauce, Jacket Potatoes with Soured Cream and Chives and a mixed green salad.

## SERVES 6

6 thin pork leg steaks

STUFFING:

2 onions, finely chopped

15 g/½ oz/1 tbsp butter

1 eating (dessert) apple, finely chopped

50 g/2 oz/1 cup fresh breadcrumbs

10 ml/2 tsp chopped sage

Salt and freshly ground black pepper

1 egg yolk

SAUCE:

30 ml/2 tbsp olive oil

450 g/1 lb tomatoes, skinned and chopped

150 ml/¼ pt/⅔ cup chicken or vegetable stock

15 ml/1 tbsp tomato purée (paste)

2.5 ml/½ tsp dried mixed herbs

Good pinch of caster (superfine) sugar

TO SERVE:

Jacket Potatoes with Soured Cream and Chives (see page 99)

Mixed green salad

# Marinated Three-flavour Ribs

These take a little time to prepare but the resulting flavours are well worth it. Try using breast of lamb, cut into ribs, for any of the marinades.

## SERVES 6

36 Chinese pork spare ribs, trimmed

30 ml/2 tbsp white wine vinegar

BARBECUE MARINADE:

30 ml/2 tbsp olive oil

1 wineglass of red wine

15 ml/1 tbsp golden (light corn) syrup

10 ml/2 tsp Worcestershire sauce

15 ml/1 tbsp tomato purée (paste)

10 ml/2 tsp red wine vinegar

1 garlic clove, crushed

Salt and freshly ground black pepper

SWEET AND SOUR MARINADE:

1 garlic clove, crushed

30 ml/2 tbsp sunflower oil

1 wineglass of pineapple juice

30 ml/2 tbsp tomato ketchup (catsup)

15 ml/1 tbsp red wine vinegar

30 ml/2 tbsp soy sauce

30 ml/2 tbsp light brown sugar

SPICY ORANGE MARINADE:

150 ml/¼ pt/⅔ cup chicken stock

Grated rind and juice of 2 oranges

1 onion, finely chopped

6 cloves

1 bay leaf

15 ml/1 tbsp olive oil

30 ml/2 tbsp clear honey

15 ml/1 tbsp white wine vinegar

1

Put the ribs in a large pan. Cover with water and add the vinegar. Bring to the boil, skim the surface, reduce the heat, cover and simmer for 30 minutes. Drain and place in three separate shallow dishes.

2

Mix the barbecue marinade ingredients together and pour over one dish of ribs. Toss to coat completely.

3

Mix the sweet and sour marinade ingredients together with a little salt and pepper and pour over a second dish of ribs. Toss.

4

Mix the spicy orange marinade ingredients with a little salt and pepper and pour over the final dish of ribs. Toss.

5

Leave all the ribs to marinate for 3–4 hours. Drain off each of the marinades into separate small saucepans. Boil rapidly until syrupy. Barbecue the ribs, keeping the different ones separate on the grill, so you can brush with the right marinade during cooking. Turn and brush frequently until golden (about 8–10 minutes). Serve with Jacket Potatoes with Prawn Dressing (see page 99) and a bean sprout, carrot and cucumber salad.

# *Siena Steaks*

Sliced aubergine (eggplant) makes a delicious addition to the topping ingredients.

**1**

*P*ut the steaks in a shallow dish in a single layer. Cover with half the sliced onion. Mix two-thirds of the oil with the remaining marinade ingredients and pour over. Leave to marinate for at least 2 hours, turning once or twice.

**2**

Meanwhile, heat the remaining oil in a saucepan. Add the remaining onion and the rest of the topping ingredients. Fry (sauté), stirring, for 2 minutes. Add 60 ml/4 tbsp of the meat marinade and simmer for 10 minutes until the vegetables are tender. Season to taste. Keep warm on the side of the barbecue.

**3**

Drain the meat and barbecue for 3–6 minutes on each side, or to taste. Transfer to plates and top with the vegetable mixture. Serve with Potato Salad Speciality and a green salad.

| SERVES 6 |
| --- |
| 6 sirloin steaks, trimmed of excess fat |
| MARINADE: |
| 2 onions, sliced |
| 45 ml/3 tbsp olive oil |
| 150 ml/¼ pt/⅔ cup red wine |
| 1 bay leaf |
| Freshly ground black pepper |
| 5 ml/1 tsp grainy mustard |
| TOPPING: |
| 1 red (bell) pepper, sliced |
| 1 green pepper, sliced |
| 1 garlic clove, crushed |
| 4 tomatoes, cut into wedges |
| 12 green olives, stoned (pitted) |
| TO SERVE: |
| Potato Salad Speciality (see page 97) |
| Green salad |

# Greek Lamb Fillets with Feta and Apricots

This is just as delicious with pork tenderloin. The stuffing and the marinade combine to make the meat wonderfully tender and full of flavour.

### SERVES 6

3 lamb neck fillets (each about 225 g/8 oz)

3 fresh apricots, stoned (pitted) and chopped

25 g/1 oz mushrooms, chopped

25 g/1 oz/¼ cup Feta cheese, crumbled

15 ml/1 tbsp chopped parsley

Salt and freshly ground black pepper

1 small egg, beaten

60 ml/4 tbsp olive oil

10 ml/2 tsp dried oregano

30 ml/2 tbsp lemon juice

10 ml/2 tsp clear honey

SPICED YOGHURT:

300 ml/½ pt/1¼ cups plain Greek-style yoghurt

5 ml/1 tsp ground cumin

2.5 ml/½ tsp chilli powder

5 ml/1 tsp ground cinnamon

Grated rind and juice of ½ lemon

10 ml/2 tsp clear honey

TO SERVE:

Village Salad (see page 96)

Greek bread

**1**

Trim any fat or gristle from the lamb. Make a slit down the length of each fillet, not cutting right through, to form a pocket.

**2**

Mix the apricots, mushrooms, cheese, parsley and a little salt and pepper together. Add enough of the beaten egg to bind the ingredients. Press into the cavities and tie securely with string.

**3**

Whisk the oil, oregano, lemon juice, honey and a little salt and pepper together in a large shallow dish. Add the stuffed lamb and turn in the marinade. Leave to marinate for at least 2 hours, turning occasionally.

**4**

Mix the spiced yoghurt ingredients together in a bowl and chill until ready to serve.

**5**

Remove the lamb from the marinade and barbecue for about 8–10 minutes on each side, turning occasionally until well browned, tender and cooked to your liking, brushing with any remaining marinade during cooking.

**6**

Remove the string and cut the fillets into thick slices. Transfer to serving plates and spoon a little of the spiced yoghurt to one side of each plate. Serve with Village Salad and Greek bread.

# Crunchy Meatballs with Tomato Barbecue Sauce

For a change, try serving these with a cold pasta salad instead of tabbouleh.

**1**

Mix all the meatball ingredients together in a large bowl. Shape into balls about the size of a golf ball and thread on to soaked wooden skewers, about four to a skewer.

**2**

To make the sauce, fry (sauté) the large chopped onion in 15 ml/1 tbsp of the oil for 3 minutes, stirring. Add the remaining sauce ingredients and simmer for 10 minutes until pulpy. Keep warm at the side of the barbecue.

**3**

Brush the meatballs with some of the remaining oil and barbecue for about 10 minutes, turning occasionally until cooked through and golden brown, brushing with a little more oil during cooking.

**4**

Garnish with lemon wedges and serve with the warm barbecue sauce and tabbouleh.

| SERVES 6 |
| --- |
| **MEATBALLS:** |
| 750 g/1½ lb minced (ground) beef, lamb or pork |
| 50 g/2 oz/1 cup fresh breadcrumbs |
| 1 onion, finely chopped |
| 2 celery sticks, finely chopped |
| 50 g/2 oz/½ cup peanuts, chopped |
| 5 ml/1 tsp ground cumin |
| 5 ml/1 tsp dried oregano |
| Salt and freshly ground black pepper |
| 1 small egg, beaten |
| **SAUCE:** |
| 1 large onion, chopped |
| 45 ml/3 tbsp olive oil |
| 400 g/14 oz/1 large can of chopped tomatoes |
| 15 ml/1 tbsp clear honey |
| 30 ml/2 tbsp sweet pickle |
| 15 ml/1 tbsp red wine vinegar |
| A few drops of Worcestershire sauce |
| **TO GARNISH:** |
| Lemon wedges |
| **TO SERVE:** |
| Tabbouleh (see page 95) |

# Sensational Side Dishes

## Wild Rice Salad

Wild rice isn't rice at all, but a grass! However, it makes an unusual and elegant accompaniment.

### SERVES 6

350 g/12 oz/1½ cups wild rice mix (a mixture of wild and long-grain rice)

1 bunch of spring onions (scallions), chopped

100 g/4 oz fresh shelled peas (about 225 g/8 oz unshelled weight)

50 g/2 oz/½ cup sunflower seeds

50 g/2 oz baby button mushrooms, sliced

FRENCH DRESSING:

45 ml/3 tbsp olive oil

15 ml/1 tbsp white wine vinegar

5 ml/1 tsp caster (superfine) sugar

5 ml/1 tsp Dijon mustard

Salt and freshly ground black pepper

TO GARNISH:

Chopped parsley

1

Cook the rice according to the packet directions. Drain, rinse with cold water and drain again.

2

Turn into a salad bowl and add the remaining ingredients. Toss gently.

3

Put the dressing ingredients in a screw-topped jar and shake thoroughly. Drizzle over, toss and chill until ready to serve, garnished with chopped parsley.

# Tabbouleh

This traditional Middle Eastern dish is even better if made one day in advance and chilled overnight to allow the flavours to develop.

**1**

Wash the wheat and put in a salad bowl with the salt. Pour the boiling water over, stir and leave to stand for 20 minutes. Stir again. The grains will have absorbed all the water.

**2**

Stir in the remaining ingredients except the cucumber, tomatoes and pepper. Leave to cool.

**3**

Add the remaining ingredients, fluff up with a fork and chill until ready to serve.

| SERVES 6 |
| --- |
| 175 g/6 oz/1½ cups bulgar (cracked) wheat |
| 5 ml/1 tsp salt |
| 325 ml/11 fl oz/1½ cups boiling water |
| 45 ml/3 tbsp olive oil |
| Grated rind and juice of 1 small lemon |
| 20 ml/4 tsp chopped mint |
| 1 garlic clove, crushed |
| 20 ml/4 tsp chopped parsley |
| 10 ml/2 tsp chopped coriander (cilantro) |
| 5 cm/2 in piece of cucumber, finely diced |
| 4 tomatoes, skinned, seeded and chopped |
| 1 small red (bell) pepper, chopped |

# Greek Village Salad

No Greek meal would be complete without a Village Salad and it is the perfect side dish for any barbecue.

## SERVES 6

¼ **small white cabbage, shredded**

½ **small iceberg lettuce, shredded**

3 **tomatoes, cut into wedges**

5 cm/2 in **piece of cucumber, diced**

1 **small onion, sliced and separated into rings**

75 g/3 oz/¾ cup **Feta cheese, roughly crumbled**

6 **black olives**

5 ml/1 tsp **dried oregano**

**Olive oil**

**Red wine vinegar**

**Salt and freshly ground black pepper**

1

_P_ut the cabbage and lettuce on a large platter. Scatter the tomatoes, cucumber, onion, cheese and olives over. Sprinkle with oregano.

2

Just before serving, drizzle with a little olive oil and vinegar and add a sprinkling of salt and a good grinding of black pepper.

# New Potato Salad with Olives and Crème Fraîche

Based on a famous dish called Jansen's Temptation, this potato salad is bursting with flavours.

### 1
Boil the potatoes in lightly salted water until just tender. Drain and place in a bowl. Leave to cool for about 15 minutes.

### 2
Mix the mayonnaise and crème fraîche together. Reserve two anchovy fillets. Chop the remainder and add to the potatoes with the mayonnaise mixture. Add the olives and toss together with a good grinding of pepper.

### 3
Sprinkle with the parsley and caraway seeds. Cut the reserved anchovy fillets into thin strips and lay in a criss-cross pattern over the top. Serve at room temperature.

| SERVES 6 |
| --- |
| 750 g/1½ lb baby new potatoes, scrubbed |
| 30 ml/2 tbsp mayonnaise |
| 30 ml/2 tbsp crème fraîche |
| 50 g/2 oz/1 small can of anchovies, drained |
| 12 black olives, stoned (pitted) and halved |
| Freshly ground black pepper |
| 15 ml/1 tbsp chopped parsley |
| 10 ml/2 tsp caraway seeds |

# Southern Grilled Potato Skins

You can buy frozen versions of these but the flavour isn't nearly as good as home-made!

| SERVES 6 |
| --- |
| 6 large potatoes, scrubbed |
| SEASONINGS: |
| 45 ml/3 tbsp sunflower oil |
| 5 ml/1 tsp garlic salt |
| 5 ml/1 tsp chilli powder |
| 5 ml/1 tsp mixed (apple-pie) spice |
| 5 ml/1 tsp ground cumin |
| Freshly ground black pepper |

1

Prick the potatoes all over with a fork. Bake in a preheated oven at 180°C/350°F/gas mark 4 for about 1 hour or until soft. Alternatively, bake in the microwave for about 4 minutes per potato (or according to the manufacturer's directions).

2

Cut the potatoes in half and scoop out most of the potato (use in a recipe needing mashed potato), leaving a 'wall' about 5 mm/¼ in thick. Cut each half into three wedges.

3

Brush all over with oil. Mix the seasonings together then sprinkle evenly over the potato skins.

4

Place on a sheet of foil, if liked. Barbecue for about 10 minutes, turning occasionally, until crisp and golden. Serve hot.

# Jacket Potatoes with a Difference

In the microwave or the oven, nothing beats a jacket potato for simplicity and versatility, but there are any number of ways to make the results imaginative.

**EACH TOPPING SERVES 6**

Prepare your jacket potatoes in the usual way (see page 98). When ready to serve, open the foil slightly, make a cross cut in the top of each potato, squeeze gently with an oven-gloved hand and top with one of the following toppings.

**Soured Cream and Chives:** Mix 300 ml/½ pt/ 1¼ cups soured (dairy sour) cream with 30 ml/2 tbsp snipped chives and some salt and freshly ground black pepper. Leave to stand for at least 1 hour to allow the flavour to develop. As an alternative, use Greek-style yoghurt and 2–4 chopped spring onions (scallions).

**Prawn Dressing:** Mix 150 ml/¼ pt/⅔ cup mayonnaise with 150 ml/¼ pt/⅔ cup plain yoghurt. Flavour to taste with tomato ketchup (catsup), lemon juice, Worcestershire sauce and cayenne. Add 100 g/4 oz/1 cup peeled, cooked prawns (shrimp) and fold in gently. Season to taste.

**Cottage Cheese with Ham and Pineapple:** Mix 200 g/7 oz/scant 1 cup cottage cheese with pineapple with two slices of ham, finely chopped, and a little salt and pepper. Garnish each with a gherkin (cornichon) fan made by slicing from the rounded end lengthways not quite through to the stalk end several times and then opening out to form a fan.

**Red Leicester and Coleslaw:** Mix 225 g/8 oz/ 1 cup coleslaw with 100 g/4 oz/1 cup grated Red Leicester cheese and a pinch of cayenne.

**Tuna and Sweetcorn Crunch:** Mix 185 g/ 6½ oz/1 small can of tuna, drained with 200 g/7 oz/1 small can of sweetcorn (corn), drained, a small green (bell) pepper, finely diced, and about 45 ml/3 tbsp mayonnaise, or enough to moisten to taste. Season with a little salt and freshly ground black pepper.

# Roasted Mediterranean Vegetables

This popular dish can be cooked in the oven but it tastes far better with that delicious, authentic barbecue flavour. See photograph on page 77.

| SERVES 6 |
| --- |
| 3 courgettes (zucchini), thickly sliced |
| 1 aubergine (eggplant), sliced |
| 1 red onion, thickly sliced and separated into rings |
| 1 red (bell) pepper, cut into 6 wedges |
| 1 green pepper, cut into 6 wedges |
| 1 yellow pepper, cut into 6 wedges |
| 30 ml/2 tbsp olive oil |
| 5 ml/1 tsp dried oregano |
| Freshly ground black pepper |
| 12 black olives |
| Coarse sea salt |

**1**

*L*ay all the prepared vegetables on a large square of oiled foil, shiny side up. Drizzle with the remaining oil and sprinkle with the oregano and some pepper. Wrap the foil over to form a parcel, twisting the edges together to seal.

**2**

Place on the barbecue for about 25 minutes, turning the parcel over once or twice, until the vegetables are just tender.

**3**

Sprinkle with the olives and some coarse sea salt and serve immediately.

# Summer Vegetable Kebabs with Passion Fruit Dressing

The passion fruit in this dressing adds an unusual and delectable fragrance.

**1**

Thread the pieces of leek, the potatoes, the courgette, the mushrooms and the tomatoes on to six skewers.

**2**

Put the oil and lemon juice in a bowl. Halve the passion fruit and scoop the seeds and pulp into the bowl. Add the honey and seasoning and whisk together. Brush a little of this dressing over the kebabs.

**3**

Barbecue for about 6–8 minutes, turning occasionally until cooked through and golden, brushing once or twice during cooking.

**4**

Remove from the skewers and drizzle the remaining dressing over. Serve straight away.

| SERVES 6 |
| --- |
| 1 leek, cut into 6 pieces and blanched |
| 12 baby new potatoes, cooked |
| 1 courgette (zucchini), cut into 6 pieces and blanched |
| 6 button mushrooms |
| 6 cherry tomatoes |
| DRESSING: |
| 45 ml/3 tbsp olive oil |
| 15 ml/1 tbsp lemon juice |
| 1 passion fruit |
| 5 ml/1 tsp clear honey |
| Salt and freshly ground black pepper |

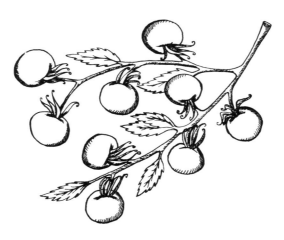

# Barbecue Desserts

# Chocolate Fondue with Fresh Fruit Dippers

Make sure you use a heavy-based pan or the chocolate will burn and crystallise.

## SERVES 6

**FONDUE:**

225 g/8 oz plain (semi-sweet) chocolate, broken into squares

300 ml/½ pt/1¼ cups single (light) cream

100 g/4 oz/⅔ cup icing (confectioners') sugar

75 g/3 oz/⅓ cup unsalted (sweet) butter

5 ml/1 tsp vanilla essence (extract)

**DIPPERS:**

12 strawberries (unhulled)

2 oranges, divided into segments

2 bananas, cut into chunks and dipped in lemon juice

6 small bunches of grapes

Shortbread fingers

**1**

Place all the fondue ingredients in a flameproof pot and heat gently, stirring until melted. Keep warm, if necessary, at the side of the barbecue (but not directly over the coals or it might burn).

**2**

Arrange the fruits on six serving plates with some shortbread fingers. When ready to serve, make sure the fondue is hot, then bring to the table and serve with forks to dip the fruits into the chocolate. Dip shortbread fingers in last to scoop up the dregs!

*Opposite: Swedish Potato Salad with Apple and Caraway (page 120)*

# Apple and Raspberry Mallow Parcels

Strawberries are equally suitable for these mouth-watering parcels, or ripe blackberries when in season.

**1**

Butter six sheets of foil, shiny sides up. Lay the apple rings neatly on top and scatter the raspberries over.

**2**

Snip the marshmallows with wet scissors and scatter over. Wrap loosely but securely in the foil.

**3**

Barbecue for 5 minutes until the apples are just cooked and the marshmallows have melted. Serve straight from the parcels with whipped cream or ice cream.

| SERVES 6 |
| --- |
| A little butter for greasing |
| 6 eating (dessert) apples, cored and cut into rings |
| 100 g/4 oz raspberries |
| 100 g/4 oz marshmallows |
| TO SERVE: |
| Whipped cream or ice cream |

*Opposite: Strawberries with Citrus Cream (page 133)*

# Butterscotch Bananas

This is a great way to use up ripe bananas with skins which are beginning to blacken.

| SERVES 6 |
| --- |
| 6 ripe bananas |
| 100 g/4 oz/½ cup butter, softened |
| 175 g/6 oz/¾ cup soft brown sugar |
| 45 ml/3 tbsp lemon juice |
| TO SERVE: |
| Greek-style yoghurt |

**1**

Cut the bananas in half first lengthways, then in half through the middle and place on six squares of lightly buttered foil, shiny sides up.

**2**

Mash the butter with the sugar and lemon juice and spread over the bananas. Wrap securely in foil. Barbecue for 3–4 minutes, turning once.

**3**

Serve straight away with Greek-style yoghurt.

# Strawberry and Apricot Croûtes

Do keep a close eye on these as they cook – the bread browns very quickly.

| SERVES 6 |
| --- |
| 4 thick slices of white or wholemeal bread, each cut into 9 cubes |
| 100 g/4 oz/½ cup butter, melted |
| 12 strawberries, hulled |
| 6 apricots, halved and stoned (pitted) |
| Caster (superfine) sugar, for sprinkling |
| TO SERVE: |
| Strawberry or apricot Greek-style yoghurt |

**1**

Dip the bread cubes in some of the melted butter and thread alternately with the fruit on to six soaked wooden skewers.

**2**

Brush the fruits with melted butter and sprinkle the kebabs with caster sugar. Barbecue for 3–4 minutes, turning occasionally until lightly golden.

**3**

Serve straight away with a spoonful of yoghurt.

# Honey-mulled Peaches or Nectarines

These are also delicious in white wine or cider, if you prefer. See photograph on page 78.

**1**

Plunge the fruit quickly into boiling water for a few seconds, then drain and peel off the skins. Leave the fruit whole.

**2**

Put the remaining ingredients in a saucepan. Place the fruit in the liquid.

**3**

Transfer to the barbecue and poach for 5–10 minutes. Spoon into serving dishes, discarding the cinnamon stick and cloves. Serve with pouring cream.

| SERVES 6 |
| --- |
| 6 large peaches or nectarines |
| 300 ml/½ pt/1¼ cups red wine |
| 150 ml/¼ pt/⅔ cup water |
| 30 ml/2 tbsp clear honey |
| 1 cinnamon stick |
| 2 cloves |
| TO SERVE: |
| Pouring cream |

# Grilled Camembert and Pineapple

Fruit and cheese always makes a delicious combination. You can use melon instead of pineapple for a change.

### SERVES 6

2 small ripe pineapples

30 ml/2 tbsp kirsch

6 individual portions of Camembert

12 small round oatcakes

**1**

Cut each pineapple into three wedges. Cut out the core, then loosen the flesh and cut into chunks, leaving on the skin.

**2**

Place on six serving plates and sprinkle 5 ml/1 tsp of kirsch over each portion.

**3**

When ready to serve, place the Camemberts on a piece of foil on the barbecue and cook for a few moments until the cheese starts to run.

**4**

Quickly transfer to the serving plates with the pineapple, add two small oatcakes to each plate and serve immediately.

# Toasted Cherry Deckers with Crème Fraîche

Apricot pie filling, sprinkled with toasted flaked (slivered) almonds, makes a delicious variation to this simple dessert.

### 1
*B*utter six slices of the bread on both sides on a board. Spread cherry pie filling over, not quite to the edge of each slice.

### 2
Butter the remaining bread on one side only and place, buttered sides up, over the cherry filling. Press the edges gently together all round the filling to seal.

### 3
Place on a hinged wire rack, close and cook until golden brown on both sides.

### 4
Meanwhile, mix the sugar and cinnamon together. Dust both sides of the sandwiches with the cinnamon sugar and place on serving plates. Top each with a dollop of crème fraîche and serve immediately.

| SERVES 6 |
| --- |
| Butter, softened |
| 12 slices white of bread, crusts removed |
| 400 g/14 oz/1 large can of cherry pie filling |
| 45 ml/3 tbsp caster (superfine) sugar |
| 10 ml/2 tsp ground cinnamon |
| TO SERVE: |
| Crème fraîche |

# Baked Chocolate and Hazelnut Pears with Brandy Cream

Peaches and nectarines bake well too, and will complement the wickedly rich brandy cream perfectly.

| SERVES 6 |
| --- |
| 6 eating (dessert) pears |
| 45 ml/3 tbsp chocolate hazelnut (filbert) spread |
| 50 g/2 oz/½ cup chopped hazelnuts |
| 3 chocolate chip cookies, crushed |
| A little butter |
| BRANDY CREAM: |
| 300 ml/½ pt/1¼ cups double (heavy) or whipping cream |
| 30 ml/2 tbsp icing (confectioners') sugar |
| 30 ml/2 tbsp brandy |

**1**
Peel the pears, then cut them in half lengthways, remove the stems and scoop out the cores.

**2**
Mix the chocolate spread with the nuts and crushed cookies. Pack into the cavities in the pears and sandwich back together.

**3**
Lightly butter six squares of foil, shiny sides up, and place a pear on each. Wrap securely in the foil.

**4**
Make the brandy cream. Whip the cream and icing sugar with the brandy until softly peaking. Chill until ready to serve.

**5**
Barbecue the pears for 10 minutes, turning occasionally, until hot through. Unwrap and serve with the whipped brandy cream.

# Simple Outdoor Eating

It's summer. The days are long and warm. It doesn't have to be a special occasion to eat outside. Whether you've come home from work, hot and shattered, or want to have a simple lunch with your family, dining in the garden makes it feel special.

In this chapter there are some simple grills you can either cook conventionally or on a foil 'instant' barbecue which is very inexpensive to buy, provides plenty of cookability even for a family and is hot and ready to use in about 10 minutes. No mess, no fuss and even worth it if you're on your own! There are also some sensational fork salads – colourful, nutritious creations in one bowl – which can be thrown together when you're ready, or made in advance and chilled. You'll also find some easy-to-eat oven-to-garden meals which can be prepared in advance, then put on automatic to cook when it suits you. And, to round everything off, some simple but fabulously effective desserts.

## KNOW-HOW

- If you have garden furniture, fine; if not, bring out a card table or a folding kitchen one and the dining chairs, if necessary.

- The fork salads are easy enough to eat lounging on a sun-bed. But it's probably better for your digestion to eat at a table!

- If you're planning to cook indoors and then have hot food outside, keep it simple and choose meals that taste good even when not piping hot, such as pasta- and rice-based ones.

- As you don't want to be slaving over a hot stove for hours, conventional roasts with lots of different pans of vegetables are best avoided. Go for a simple salad accompaniment instead.

- Mosquitoes and other biting insects can be a problem in the evenings, as can wasps during the day. Burning candles on the table can help; you can buy ones especially for use outdoors at most garden centres and supermarkets.

# Top Tips

To enjoy a quick barbecue in the evening, keep a bottle of basic marinade in the fridge, drizzle some over chops, steaks, sausages or whatever you fancy before you go to work in the morning. Leave to marinate in the fridge all day.

**Basic marinade:** 4 parts olive oil to 2 parts wine or cider or 1 part wine or cider vinegar, a good pinch of caster (superfine) sugar, some salt and freshly ground black pepper and a few pinches of dried mixed herbs. Vary the flavour by using different herbs or a spice such as chilli powder, cumin or ground coriander (cilantro).

When you get home, light the 'instant' barbecue, pour yourself a drink and have a quick shower while the coals heat up. Then you're ready to throw the meat on at your convenience! Just like a normal barbecue, the coals stay hot for a long time – there will be plenty of heat to cook a meal for four people.

Note: Make sure the foil barbecue is on a fireproof surface, such as concrete. Don't put it straight on the lawn or you'll have a burnt patch!

If you're on your own, don't waste the heat. Cook some sausages, chicken, fish or gammon that you could then enjoy cold the following evening. Likewise, if you're making a fork salad or an oven-to-garden meal, although all the recipes are easily divisible by four, make half the quantity: it will keep in the fridge for up to three days so you've got two meals for one lot of effort!

# Drinks

Anything goes – whatever you'd normally drink is fine. Cold beers, lagers and cider are always popular. Iced sparkling soft drinks, chilled juices or mineral water go down well too. A wine box is useful if you enjoy a glass with your meal. If you like white or rosé wine, try to keep the box in the fridge to keep it chilled. Alternatively, if space is tight, keep it in a cool box with an ice pack. Keep a second ice pack in the freezer so you can replace one as it thaws.

# Meals from the Grill

# Lamb Steaks with Garlic, Rosemary and Redcurrant

You can use chops instead of steaks, but remember, most people can easily eat two!

### SERVES 4

4 lamb leg steaks

1 garlic clove, crushed

30 ml/2 tbsp olive oil

15 ml/1 tbsp lemon juice

15 ml/1 tbsp redcurrant jelly (clear conserve)

5 ml/1 tsp dried rosemary

Salt and freshly ground black pepper

TO SERVE:

New potatoes

Tomato and onion salad

**1**

Wipe the steaks, clean with kitchen paper (paper towels), then place them in a single layer in a large shallow dish.

**2**

Whisk the remaining ingredients together and pour over the meat. Leave to marinate for at least 2 hours.

**3**

Grill (broil) or barbecue for 5 minutes on each side until tender, turning once or twice and brushing with the marinade during cooking.

**4**

Serve with a bowl of hot new potatoes and a tomato and onion salad.

# Pork with Tangy Tomato Sauce

Turkey, chicken and sausages all taste wonderful with the sauce in this recipe.

**1**

Wipe the chops and carefully trim off any excess fat, cutting to a neat shape.

**2**

Mix the sauce ingredients together in a small bowl. Brush all over the chops and grill (broil) or barbecue for 15–20 minutes, turning occasionally and brushing frequently with the sauce until stickily coated, browned and cooked through. (The time will depend on the thickness of the chops.)

NOTE: If liked, make more of the sauce to serve as an accompaniment to the chops or any grilled meats or poultry.

| SERVES 4 |
| --- |
| 4 pork chops |
| SAUCE: |
| 30 ml/2 tbsp tomato ketchup (catsup) |
| 5 ml/1 tsp Worcestershire sauce |
| 15 ml/1 tbsp clear honey or golden (light corn) syrup |
| 15 ml/1 tbsp vinegar |
| Dash of soy sauce (optional) |
| TO SERVE: |
| Plain boiled rice |
| Green salad |

# Grilled Italian Platter

If you don't like anchovies, add some thin slices of pancetta to the aubergine. Make sure they are sizzling hot before serving.

### SERVES 4

1 fennel bulb, cut lengthways into 5 mm/¼ in slices

2 small courgettes (zucchini), cut lengthways into 5 mm/¼ in slices

1 small aubergine (eggplant), cut lengthways into 5 mm/¼ in slices

2 onions, quartered

1 red (bell) pepper, quartered

400 g/14 oz/1 large can of artichoke bottoms, drained

4 large open mushrooms, peeled

MARINADE:

60 ml/4 tbsp olive oil

1 garlic clove, crushed

Grated rind and juice of 1 lime

Salt and freshly ground black pepper

50 g/2 oz/1 small can of anchovies, drained

30 ml/2 tbsp milk

100 g/4 oz Mozzarella, cut into 4 slices

TO GARNISH:

15 ml/1 tbsp chopped parsley

TO SERVE:

Ciabatta

1

Cook the fennel in boiling, lightly salted water for 3 minutes. Drain thoroughly, rinse with cold water and drain again.

2

Arrange all the prepared vegetables in a large shallow roasting tin (pan).

3

Mix together the marinade ingredients, except the anchovies, milk and Mozzarella, and drizzle over the vegetables. Toss gently.

4

Soak the anchovies in the milk.

5

Place all the vegetables on the grill (broiler) rack or barbecue and cook, turning and brushing with any remaining marinade until golden and tender – about 6 minutes. Lay a slice of Mozzarella on each of the mushrooms and the anchovy strips over the aubergines for the last minute or so of cooking until the anchovies are hot and the cheese is melting. Do not turn again.

6

Transfer everything to warm serving plates, sprinkle with chopped parsley and serve with ciabatta.

# Honey Mustard Sausages with Beefsteak Tomatoes

Try varying the kinds of sausages you use – we all tend to choose pork, but turkey sausages are particularly good barbecued like this.

### 1

Mix the honey and mustard. Separate the sausages and place on a grill (broiler) rack, or barbecue with the tomato halves, cut sides down. Brush the sausages with the honey mixture.

### 2

Grill (broil) the sausages for 10 minutes, turning and brushing frequently with the honey mustard mixture, until browned and cooked through.

### 3

After 3 minutes' cooking, turn the tomatoes up the other way. Spread the purée over the top, sprinkle with the basil, then the cheese. Continue cooking until the tomatoes are tender and the cheese has melted.

### 4

Serve the sausages and tomatoes with fluffy creamed potatoes and a green salad.

| SERVES 4 |
| --- |
| 15 ml/1 tbsp clear honey |
| 15 ml/1 tbsp Dijon mustard |
| 900 g/2 lb large, good-quality pork sausages |
| 4 beefsteak tomatoes, halved |
| 20 ml/4 tsp tomato purée (paste) |
| 5 ml/1 tsp dried basil |
| 50 g/2 oz/½ cup Cheddar cheese, grated |
| TO SERVE: |
| Fluffy creamed potatoes |
| Green salad |

# Spicy Coconut Yoghurt Chicken Breasts

White fish is excellent cooked in this way, but you will need to use a hinged wire rack or place it on foil and allow only 4–5 minutes per side.

### SERVES 4

120 ml/4 fl oz/½ cup plain yoghurt

20 ml/4 tsp mild curry paste

20 ml/4 tsp desiccated (shredded) coconut

15 ml/1 tbsp light brown sugar

Salt and freshly ground black pepper

10 ml/2 tsp chopped coriander (cilantro)

4 chicken breasts

TO SERVE:

Plain boiled rice

TO GARNISH:

Lemon wedges

Shredded lettuce

Sliced cucumber and tomato

1

Mix together the yoghurt, curry paste, coconut, sugar, a little salt and pepper and the coriander. Add the chicken breasts and turn to coat completely. Leave to marinate for as long as possible (up to 12 hours).

2

Remove from the marinade and place on a grill (broiler) rack or barbecue. Grill (broil) or barbecue for 10–15 minutes, turning occasionally and brushing with any remaining marinade until cooked through and golden.

3

Serve on a bed of boiled rice, garnished with lemon wedges, shredded lettuce, sliced cucumber and tomato.

# Trout with Horseradish and Almond Butter

Try this with mackerel too – excellent!

1

Slash the fish on both sides several times with a sharp knife. This helps the flavoured butter to penetrate the flesh.

2

Mash the butter and horseradish together and spread a little over four sheets of foil, shiny sides up, and sprinkle with half the almonds.

3

Lay a fish on top of each sheet and spread with the remaining butter mixture. Sprinkle with the remaining nuts, the parsley and a little salt and pepper.

4

Wrap loosely but securely and grill (broil) or barbecue for 12–15 minutes, turning once, until the fish is cooked through.

5

Transfer to serving plates and serve hot, garnished with lemon wedges. Serve with new potatoes and a green bean salad.

| SERVES 4 |
| --- |
| 4 trout, cleaned |
| 75 g/3 oz/⅓ cup unsalted (sweet) butter |
| 20 ml/4 tsp horseradish sauce |
| 30 ml/2 tbsp flaked (slivered) almonds |
| 20 ml/4 tsp chopped parsley |
| Salt and freshly ground black pepper |
| TO GARNISH: |
| Lemon wedges |
| TO SERVE: |
| New potatoes |
| Cold cooked French (green) beans, tossed in French dressing and sprinkled with very finely chopped onion |

# Fork Salads

## Swedish Potato Salad with Apple and Caraway

For added bite, sprinkle some crisp garlic croûtons over the salad just before serving. See photograph on page 103.

| SERVES 4 |
|---|
| 450 g/1 lb baby new potatoes, scrubbed and halved |
| 4 rollmop herrings, sliced |
| 1 red eating (dessert) apple, diced |
| 5 cm/2 in piece of cucumber, diced |
| 200 g/7 oz/1 small can of sweetcorn (corn), drained |
| 5 ml/1 tsp caraway seeds |
| 150 ml/¼ pt/⅔ cup soured (dairy sour) cream |
| 30 ml/2 tbsp milk |
| Salt and freshly ground black pepper |
| TO GARNISH: |
| 1 onion, sliced and separated into rings |
| 4 gherkins (cornichons), sliced |

1

Cook the potatoes in boiling, lightly salted water until tender. Drain, rinse with cold water, drain again and turn into a bowl.

2

Add the remaining ingredients except the soured cream, milk and seasonings and toss gently.

3

Blend the cream and milk together with a little salt and pepper. Pour over the salad and toss gently so as not to break up the fish. Pile on to serving plates and garnish with onion rings and sliced gherkins.

# *Biryani Salad*

Cooked lamb can be used instead of chicken. Toss in any left-over cooked carrots, peas, beans, broccoli or cauliflower too!

**1**

Cook the rice according to the packet directions. Drain, rinse with cold water and drain again. Leave to cool.

**2**

Place in a salad bowl and add the remaining ingredients. Toss gently.

**3**

Whisk the dressing ingredients together with a little salt and pepper. Pour over the salad and toss gently.

**4**

Turn into serving bowls and garnish each with a sprinkling of currants and toasted almonds.

| SERVES 4 |
| --- |
| 200 g/7 oz/1 packet of pilau rice |
| 175 g/6 oz/1½ cups cooked chicken, diced |
| 430 g/15½ oz/1 large can of chick peas (garbanzos), drained |
| 1 small green (bell) pepper, diced |
| 2 tomatoes, diced |
| 1 bunch of spring onions (scallions), chopped |
| DRESSING: |
| 90 ml/6 tbsp coconut milk |
| 90 ml/6 tbsp plain yoghurt |
| 1 small green chilli, finely chopped (or chilli powder to taste) |
| 30 ml/2 tbsp sunflower oil |
| 10 ml/2 tsp lemon juice |
| 20 ml/4 tsp smooth mango chutney |
| Salt and freshly ground black pepper |
| TO GARNISH: |
| 30 ml/2 tbsp currants |
| 30 ml/2 tbsp toasted flaked (slivered) almonds |

# Crispy Pork and Nectarine Salad with Garlic Croûtons

Smoked turkey and chicken are also tasty in this crisp and crunchy salad.

| SERVES 4 |
| --- |
| 4 ripe nectarines, skinned, stoned (pitted) and sliced |
| 100 g/4 oz smoked pork loin, cut into thin strips |
| 250 g/9 oz bean sprouts |
| 4 spring onions (scallions), cut into diagonal slices |
| 1 green (bell) pepper, cut into thin strips |
| 2 celery sticks, sliced |
| 30 ml/2 tbsp sunflower seeds |
| DRESSING: |
| 30 ml/2 tbsp sunflower oil |
| 15 ml/1 tbsp orange juice |
| 10 ml/2 tsp lemon juice |
| 5 ml/1 tsp caster (superfine) sugar |
| 5 ml/1 tsp Dijon mustard |
| TO GARNISH: |
| 2 slices of bread, cubed |
| A little oil |
| 1 garlic clove, chopped |

1

*P*ut all the prepared salad ingredients in a bowl and toss gently. Leave in a cool place if you are not serving straight away.

2

Whisk the dressing ingredients together.

3

Fry (sauté) the bread cubes in a little oil with the garlic added until golden brown. Drain on kitchen paper (paper towels). When ready to serve, pour the dressing over the salad. Toss gently, pile into bowls and garnish with the garlic croûtons.

# Red Salmon and Conchiglie Salad

This makes a can of salmon go a long way. For a delicious variation, use cheese- or mushroom-stuffed tortellini instead of pasta shells.

**1**

Cook the pasta according to the packet directions. Drain, rinse with cold water and drain again. Turn into a bowl.

**2**

Remove the skin and any bones from the salmon. Break into chunky pieces and add to the pasta.

**3**

Add the remaining ingredients and toss very gently.

**4**

Whisk the dressing ingredients together and pour over the salad. Toss gently. Fill salad bowls with some watercress. Pile the salad on top and serve, sprinkled with snipped chives.

| SERVES 4 |
| --- |
| 225 g/8 oz conchiglie (pasta shells) |
| 185 g/6½ oz/1 small can of red salmon, drained |
| 50 g/2 oz button mushrooms, sliced |
| 5 cm/2 in piece of cucumber, diced |
| 8 cherry tomatoes, halved |
| DRESSING: |
| 45 ml/3 tbsp olive oil |
| Finely grated rind and juice of 1 lime |
| 5 ml/1 tsp caster (superfine) sugar |
| 5 ml/1 tsp dried dill (dill weed) |
| 20 ml/4 tsp single (light) cream |
| TO SERVE: |
| Watercress |
| 15 ml/1 tbsp snipped chives |

# Stir-fry Vegetable and Noodle Salad

The wonderful thing about stir-fried vegetables is that they retain their 'crunch' without being hard and unappetising. Their flavours are enhanced too.

| SERVES 4 |
| --- |

75 g/3 oz/1 slab of Chinese egg noodles

45 ml/3 tbsp sunflower oil

1 bunch of spring onions (scallions), cut into diagonal pieces

1 garlic clove, crushed

1 red (bell) pepper, cut into strips

2 celery sticks, cut into matchsticks

1 large carrot, cut into matchsticks

1 courgette (zucchini), cut into matchsticks

7.5 cm/3 in piece of cucumber, cut into matchsticks

50 g/2 oz button mushrooms, sliced

15 ml/1 tbsp white wine vinegar

2.5 ml/½ tsp ground ginger

30 ml/2 tbsp soy sauce

5 ml/1 tsp caster (superfine) sugar

15 ml/1 tbsp dry sherry

Salt and freshly ground black pepper

TO SERVE:

Prawn crackers

1

Cook the noodles according to the packet directions. Drain thoroughly, rinse with cold water and drain again.

2

Heat the oil in a wok or large frying pan (skillet). Stir-fry the onions and garlic for 1 minute. Add the remaining vegetables and stir-fry for 3 minutes until slightly softened but still with 'bite'. Remove the wok or pan from the heat.

3

Add the remaining ingredients and the cooked noodles and toss well. Leave to cool.

4

Pile into bowls and serve with prawn crackers.

# Pesto and Feta Tagliarini with Poached Eggs

This is a brilliant blend of textures and flavours. Try using red pesto or tapenade instead of the more usual green pesto sauce.

**1**

Cook the pasta according to the packet directions. Add the beans halfway through cooking. Drain and return to the saucepan. Add the pesto to taste and toss gently to coat.

**2**

Poach the eggs in water for 3–5 minutes or to your liking. Drain and place in cold water to prevent further cooking and the yolks hardening.

**3**

Meanwhile, fry (sauté) the onion and garlic in the oil for 3 minutes until softened but not browned. Add the bacon and fry for a further 2 minutes, stirring.

**4**

Add the contents of the pan to the pasta and beans with the vinegar, a little salt and pepper and the cheese. Toss gently. Pile on to serving plates and top each with a poached egg. Serve straight away.

| SERVES 4 |
| --- |
| 350 g/12 oz tagliarini |
| 225 g/8 oz French beans, cut into 3 pieces |
| 30–45 ml/2–3 tbsp ready-made pesto sauce |
| 4 eggs |
| 1 Spanish onion, halved and thinly sliced |
| 1 garlic clove, finely chopped |
| 45 ml/3 tbsp olive oil |
| 4 rashers (slices) of streaky bacon, rinded and finely chopped |
| 15 ml/1 tbsp red wine vinegar |
| Salt and freshly ground black pepper |
| 100 g/4 oz/1 cup Feta cheese, crumbled |

## Speedy Seafood Lasagne ❄

This is an ideal storecupboard standby with loads of flavour.

| SERVES 4 |
| --- |

400 g/14 oz/1 large can of chopped tomatoes

2.5 ml/½ tsp dried basil

1 garlic clove, crushed

185 g/6½ oz/1 small can of tuna, drained

170 g/6 oz/1 small can of prawns (shrimp), drained

250 g/9 oz/1 small can of mussels, drained

Freshly ground black pepper

6–8 sheets of no-need-to-precook lasagne

225 g/8 oz frozen chopped spinach, thawed

298 g/10½ oz/1 small can of condensed celery soup

25 g/1 oz/¼ cup Cheddar cheese, grated

TO SERVE:

Green salad

1

Empty the contents of the can of tomatoes into a pan and add the basil and garlic. Bring to the boil and boil rapidly for 3 minutes until pulpy.

2

Stir in the tuna, prawns and mussels. Season with pepper.

3

Spoon a little of the seafood mixture in the base of a fairly shallow 1.2 litre/2 pt/5 cup ovenproof dish. Top with a layer of lasagne sheets, breaking them to fit, then half the remaining seafood mixture, then half the thawed spinach. Repeat the layers and finish with a layer of lasagne.

4

Spoon the soup over the top and sprinkle with the cheese.

5

Bake in a preheated oven at 190°C/375°F/gas mark 5 for 40 minutes until golden on top and cooked through. Serve hot with salad.

# Summer Vegetable Moussaka

For extra protein to satisfy hefty appetites, add a 425 g/15 oz can of drained cannellini beans to the mixture with the olives and wine.

**1**

Cook the potatoes in lightly salted, boiling water for about 5 minutes or until just tender. Drain thoroughly and set aside.

**2**

Meanwhile, fry (sauté) the prepared vegetables in the olive oil, stirring, for 3 minutes.

**3**

Add the olives, wine, herbs, sugar and a little salt and pepper. Reduce the heat, part-cover and simmer for 10 minutes until tender.

**4**

Layer the potatoes and vegetable mixture in a 1.5 litre/ 2½ pt/6 cup ovenproof dish, finishing with a layer of potatoes. Beat the yoghurt and egg together with a little salt and pepper and stir in the cheese. Spoon over the potatoes and bake in a preheated oven at 190°C/375°F/gas mark 5 for about 40 minutes until the topping is set and golden brown. Serve warm with a green salad.

| SERVES 4 |
| --- |
| 450 g/1 lb potatoes, sliced |
| 2 courgettes (zucchini), sliced |
| 1 aubergine (eggplant), sliced |
| 1 red (bell) pepper, cut into strips |
| 1 green pepper, cut into strips |
| 1 large onion, chopped |
| 4 tomatoes, chopped |
| 30 ml/2 tbsp olive oil |
| 12 black olives, stoned (pitted) and sliced |
| 30 ml/2 tbsp red wine |
| 5 ml/1 tsp dried mixed herbs |
| Good pinch of caster (superfine) sugar |
| Salt and freshly ground black pepper |
| 150 ml/¼ pt/⅔ cup plain yoghurt |
| 1 egg, beaten |
| 75 g/3 oz/¾ cup Cheddar cheese, grated |
| TO SERVE: |
| Green salad |

# Italian Pancetta and Fresh Pea Risotto ✳

This simple, one-pot dish tastes very good cold, too, and so can be prepared well in advance, if necessary.

| SERVES 4–6 |
| --- |
| 350 g/12 oz/1½ cups risotto rice |
| 50 g/2 oz/¼ cup butter |
| 225 g/8 oz frozen or fresh shelled peas |
| 100 g/4 oz pancetta (or streaky bacon), diced |
| 15 ml/1 tbsp chopped mint |
| 2.5 ml/½ tsp ground nutmeg |
| 750 ml/1¼ pts/3 cups chicken or vegetable stock |
| Salt and freshly ground black pepper |
| 60 ml/4 tbsp single (light) cream |
| TO SERVE: |
| Sun-dried tomato focaccia |
| Chicory and watercress salad |

**1**

Wash and drain the rice thoroughly. This removes some of the excess starch and helps to stop the grains from sticking together too much.

**2**

Melt the butter in a flameproof casserole (Dutch oven) and fry (sauté) the rice, peas and pancetta for 2 minutes, stirring.

**3**

Stir in the mint, nutmeg and stock and bring to the boil. Season lightly, cover and cook in a preheated oven at 160°C/325°F/gas mark 3 for 20 minutes or until the rice is tender and has absorbed the liquid.

**4**

Stir in the cream: the risotto should look moist and glistening. Serve straight away with sun-dried tomato focaccia and a chicory and watercress salad.

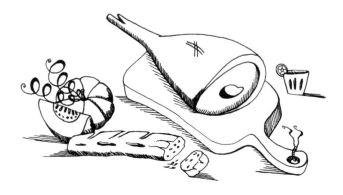

# Tuna and Fennel Coulibiac *

Coulibiac is a traditional Russian dish made with salmon which you can, of course, use instead of the tuna, if you prefer.

**1**

Fry (sauté) the fennel and onion in the butter for about 3 minutes, stirring until softened and slightly golden.

**2**

Remove from the heat and stir in the tuna, sweetcorn, mayonnaise, parsley and seasoning.

**3**

Unroll the pastry on to a dampened baking sheet. Spoon the filling down the centre. Make horizontal slits in the pastry at 2 cm/¾ in intervals down both sides to within 2.5 cm/1 in of the filling.

**4**

Fold the pastry ends over the filling, then lift the strips of pastry up over the filling from alternate sides to form a plait.

**5**

Brush with beaten egg to glaze and sprinkle with the fennel or poppy seeds. Bake in a preheated oven at 220°C/425°F/gas mark 7 for about 25 minutes until golden brown. Serve hot or cold with a cucumber salad.

| SERVES 4 |
| --- |
| 1 fennel bulb, chopped |
| 1 onion, chopped |
| 15 g/½ oz/1 tbsp butter |
| 185 g/6½ oz/1 small can of tuna, drained |
| 200 g/7 oz/1 small can of Mexican sweetcorn (corn with bell peppers) |
| 45 ml/3 tbsp mayonnaise |
| 15 ml/1 tbsp chopped parsley |
| Salt and freshly ground black pepper |
| 375 g/13 oz frozen ready-rolled puff pastry (paste), thawed |
| Beaten egg to glaze |
| 10 ml/2 tsp fennel or poppy seeds |
| TO SERVE: |
| Cucumber salad |

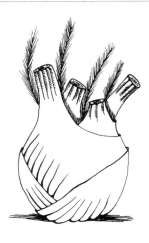

# Swiss Gruyère, Potato and Garlic Layer

Ring the changes with slices of pepperoni or salami instead of ham. If you're feeling really adventurous use half sweet potatoes.

| SERVES 4 |
| --- |
| 50 g/2 oz/¼ cup butter |
| 2 onions, sliced |
| 1 large garlic clove, crushed |
| 750 g/1½ lb potatoes, sliced |
| 6 thin slices of ham |
| 100 g/4 oz/1 cup Gruyère (Swiss) cheese, grated |
| Salt and freshly ground black pepper |
| 2 eggs |
| 300 ml/½ pt/1¼ cups milk or single (light) cream |
| TO SERVE: |
| Mixed salad |

**1**

*L*ightly grease a 1.5 litre/2½ pt/6 cup fairly shallow ovenproof dish with about one-third of the butter.

**2**

Melt the remainder in a frying pan (skillet) and fry (sauté) the onions and garlic for 2 minutes to soften.

**3**

Put a layer of about a quarter of the potatoes in the base of the dish. Spread about a third of the onion and butter mixture over, then top with two slices of the ham. Season lightly and sprinkle with about a quarter of the cheese. Repeat the layers and finish with a layer of potatoes, topped with the remaining cheese.

**4**

Whisk the eggs and milk or cream together and pour over. Bake in a preheated oven at 180°C/350°F/gas mark 4 for 1¼ hours or until the potatoes are tender and the top is golden brown. Serve hot or cold with a mixed salad.

# Neapolitan Stuffed Marrows ✳

Use this mixture to stuff (bell) peppers for another dish which you can roast in the same way.

### 1
Cook the rice in plenty of boiling, lightly salted water for 10 minutes. Drain thoroughly and return to the saucepan.

### 2
Add the canned tomatoes, the garlic, if using, the basil and tomato purée and season to taste.

### 3
Halve the marrows lengthways and scoop out the seeds. Lay in a roasting tin (pan) containing enough cold water to cover the base of the tin.

### 4
Spoon the rice mixture into the marrows. Cover the tin with foil and bake in a preheated oven at 190°C/375°F/gas mark 5 for 50 minutes. Remove the foil and top with the sliced Mozzarella. Return to the oven and cook for a further 5–10 minutes until the cheese is melted and bubbling.

### 5
Transfer to serving plates and serve with mushroom focaccia and a lettuce, cucumber and antipasto salad.

| SERVES 4 |
| --- |
| 225 g/8 oz/1 cup long-grain rice |
| 400 g/14 oz/1 large can of chopped tomatoes |
| 1 garlic clove, crushed (optional) |
| 30 ml/2 tbsp chopped basil |
| 15 ml/1 tbsp tomato purée (paste) |
| Salt and freshly ground black pepper |
| 2 young marrows (about 450 g/1 lb each) |
| 225 g/8 oz Mozzarella cheese, sliced |
| TO GARNISH: |
| Sprigs of basil |
| TO SERVE: |
| Mushroom focaccia |
| Lettuce and cucumber, topped with a drained jar of Italian vegetable antipasto and drizzled with olive oil |

# Simply Effective Desserts

## Bananas and Pears with Mocha-cream Sauce

The glorious sauce in this dish is also wonderful served over ice cream and is a great favourite with the children!

| SERVES 4 |
| --- |
| 2 large bananas |
| 2 ripe pears |
| Lemon juice |
| SAUCE: |
| 175 g/6 oz plain (semi-sweet) chocolate |
| 5 ml/1 tsp instant coffee powder |
| 25 g/1 oz/2 tbsp butter |
| 15 ml/1 tbsp golden (light corn) syrup |
| 5 ml/1 tsp vanilla essence (extract) |
| 60 ml/4 tbsp single (light) cream |

**1**

Peel and cut the bananas and pears into chunky pieces and toss in a little lemon juice to prevent browning. Divide between four serving dishes.

**2**

Break up the chocolate and place in a saucepan with the remaining ingredients except the cream. Heat gently, stirring until melted, but do not allow to boil.

**3**

Remove from the heat and beat in the cream. Use hot or cold, spooned over the fruit.

# Strawberries with Citrus Cream

For a special occasion, flavour the cream with a dash (or two!) of orange liqueur.
See photograph on page 104.

**1**

*P*ut the strawberries in a bowl and drizzle with the vinegar. Sprinkle with half the caster sugar and toss gently to combine. Leave to macerate for several hours, if possible.

**2**

Whip the cream until softly peaking. Gently whisk in the fruit rinds and juices and the remaining sugar. Chill, if time allows. Serve the fruit spooned into serving bowls, topped with the cream.

| SERVES 4 |
| --- |
| 450 g/1 lb strawberries, hulled |
| 10 ml/2 tsp balsamic vinegar |
| 30 ml/2 tbsp caster (superfine) sugar |
| CITRUS CREAM: |
| 300 ml/½ pt/1¼ cups double (heavy) cream |
| Finely grated rind and juice of 1 lime |
| Finely grated rind and juice of 1 orange |

# Chocolate Soufflé Omelette

Lemon curd makes another sensational filling for a sweet soufflé omelette.

| SERVES 1 |
| --- |
| 2 eggs, separated |
| 15 ml/1 tbsp water |
| 10 ml/2 tsp cocoa (unsweetened chocolate) powder |
| 15 ml/1 tbsp caster (superfine) sugar |
| Small knob of butter |
| 15–30 ml/1–2 tbsp chocolate hazelnut spread |
| Icing (confectioners') sugar |
| Whipped cream |

**1**

Beat the egg yolks with the water, cocoa powder and caster sugar until smooth, making sure there are no lumps.

**2**

Whisk the egg whites until stiff and fold in with a metal spoon.

**3**

Melt the butter in a small omelette pan. Add the mixture and fry (sauté) until the base is browned and set.

**4**

Place the pan under a hot grill (broiler) until the omelette is risen and set on top.

**5**

Gently spread the chocolate spread over half the omelette. (If it won't spread, dot it over the surface and return to the grill briefly to melt.) Fold in half and slide on to a serving plate.

**6**

Dust with sifted icing sugar and serve straight away with whipped cream.

# Melon and Ginger Trifles

For another quick treat, slice bananas into individual dishes, top with the ginger cake and finish in the same way.

### 1
*P*ut the melon halves into four individual dishes. If you have larger melons, you can cut them into quarters.

### 2
Break up the ginger cake and place in the melon cavities.

### 3
Moisten with ginger wine or orange juice to taste.

### 4
Chill until ready to serve, then whip the cream until peaking and whisk in the custard. Use to fill a piping bag, fitted with a large star tube, and pipe a large rosette on top of each or spoon the mixture on and swirl with the end of the spoon. Sprinkle with crystallised ginger. Decorate with a few angelica 'leaves'.

| SERVES 4 |
| --- |
| 2 small galia or other round melons, halved and seeded |
| 2 slices of slab ginger cake |
| Ginger wine or orange juice |
| 150 ml/¼ pt/⅔ cup double (heavy) cream |
| 1 small individual carton of ready-to-eat custard |
| 20 ml/4 tsp crystallised (candied) ginger, chopped |
| Angelica 'leaves' |

# Brandied Crunch Cream

This dish has been known under a number of names: Eton Mess, Cambridge Cream and Victorian Cream, to name just three.

| SERVES 4 |
| --- |
| 50 g/2 oz/⅓ cup raisins |
| 45 ml/3 tbsp brandy |
| 300 ml/½ pt/1¼ cups double (heavy) cream |
| 300 ml/½ pt/1¼ cups thick plain yoghurt |
| 30 ml/2 tbsp sifted icing (confectioners') sugar |
| 4 meringue nests, crushed |
| TO DECORATE: |
| A few chopped pistachio nuts |

1
Mix the raisins and brandy together and leave to soak for at least 1 hour until the raisins are plump and juicy.

2
Whip the cream and yoghurt together until peaking, then fold in the sugar. Fold in the brandied raisins and the crushed meringues.

3
Spoon into individual glass dishes and sprinkle with pistachio nuts before serving.

# Sparkling Blueberry Dessert

Use raspberries, loganberries or sliced strawberries or any other soft fruit in season.

| SERVES 4 |
| --- |
| 450 g/1 lb blueberries |
| 15 ml/1 tbsp chopped mint |
| 15 ml/1 tbsp caster (superfine) sugar |
| ½ bottle of sweet sparkling white wine |
| 4 scoops of vanilla ice cream |
| TO DECORATE: |
| Sprigs of mint |

1
Put the blueberries into a bowl. Sprinkle with the mint and sugar, toss gently and leave to macerate for several hours, if time allows.

2
Spoon into four large wine goblets. When ready to serve, top with sparkling wine and a scoop of ice cream. Decorate each with a sprig of mint and serve straight away.

# Garden Parties

A drinks and nibbles party in the open air is one of the most delightful ways of entertaining a lot of people and the same food is ideal whether it is lunchtime or the evening and whatever the occasion, be it a special birthday, christening, wedding reception, anniversary or charity event. Here you'll find lots of interesting and unusual sweet and savoury finger food, plus tips on how much to serve and what to offer to drink.

# KNOW-HOW

- Numbers are important. How many people you can invite depends on how big your garden is. You want enough to 'buzz' but not so many that people can't move! Bear in mind parking facilities, too, and either invite the neighbours or clear it with them first so they won't object to the noise or people parking in front of their houses. For absolute peace of mind about the weather, hire a marquee (look in *Yellow Pages* or your local paper for a supplier). An alternative is to erect a large awning, as shelter in case it rains or is blisteringly hot. If you can't do either of these, make sure there is enough room inside to accommodate everyone if needs be.

- You don't have to have enough chairs and tables for everyone to sit down, but make sure you have at least one table for the food and drink, and a few scattered around for people to put their glasses on. Some seating should be available, too, for those who don't like to stand for too long.

- Background music isn't strictly necessary, but if you do have some make sure the equipment is protected in case it rains.

- You can plan to have the food constantly being offered round amongst the guests (by hired help or you and a few chosen helpers). Alternatively, have the food dotted around and insist people help themselves. The same applies to the drinks – it can be a free-for-all or the more formal waiter service. If you are asking people to help themselves, you will still need to keep checking that they are not being reticent about it.

- If the food is out in the open, don't put it out until the guests arrive or it may start to deteriorate.

- Keep any food you want to serve warm loosely covered (not wrapped) in foil in a very low oven, until ready to serve.

- Supplement the home-made food with bowls of crisps (potato chips), nuts, olives and gherkins (cornichons).

- Allow about eight to ten nibbles per person (plus crisps, etc.).

# *Drinks*

There are basically four choices. You can either have:

- A mixed bar with a selection of spirits, mixers, sherry, vermouth, beer and soft drinks; OR

- A real 'cocktail party' with a choice of cocktails – usually one dry like a dry martini (1–2 measures of gin, 1 measure dry vermouth and a sliver of lemon peel or an olive) or a brandy sour (1–2 measures brandy and juice of ½ lemon over ice, topped up with sparkling mineral water or soda) with one sweet like a daiquiri (1 measure white rum and the juice of ½ lime, sweetened to taste with caster (superfine) sugar, over cracked ice in a frosted glass) or a sweet martini (like a dry martini but made with sweet, red vermouth) and one non-alcoholic (see Hampers with Style, page 35); OR

- A choice of sparkling wine or champagne straight or as Bucks Fizz (with orange juice) or as a cocktail (with a tiny cube of sugar in the base, a splash of Angostura bitters and a dash of brandy) or sparkling soft drinks; OR

- A choice of wines, beer or soft drinks.

**A guide to quantities:**

- A bottle of spirits will yield 28 single measures.

- A bottle of wine will yield six glasses.

- A bottle of sparkling wine or champagne will yield six to eight glasses.

- A bottle of sherry will yield 15 glasses.

# Summer Savouries

# Baby Smoked Salmon Blinis

Blinis are traditionally served with real caviare and soured (dairy sour) cream. These bite-sized versions are perfectly complemented by the smoked salmon.

| MAKES 24 |
| --- |

**PANCAKES:**

350 g/12 oz/3 cups plain (all-purpose) flour

10 ml/2 tsp easy-blend dried yeast

Pinch of salt

10 ml/2 tsp caster (superfine) sugar

375 ml/13 fl oz/1½ cups hand-hot water

2 eggs, separated

300 ml/½ pt/1¼ cups hand-hot milk

25 g/1 oz/2 tbsp butter, melted

Oil

**FILLING:**

200 g/7 oz/scant 1 cup medium-fat soft cheese

100 g/4 oz smoked salmon pieces, finely chopped

Lemon juice

Freshly ground black pepper

50 g/2 oz/1 small jar of Danish lumpfish roe

**1**

Sift the flour into a bowl and stir in the yeast, salt and sugar. Mix with the water to a thick batter. Cover and leave in a warm place for 30 minutes.

**2**

Whisk the egg yolks and milk together and whisk into the batter with the butter. Whisk the egg whites until stiff and fold in with a metal spoon.

**3**

Heat a little oil in a frying pan (skillet) and make three pancakes, using 10 ml/2 tsp of the batter for each one. Cook for 1 minute on each side until golden. Wrap in a clean cloth while making the remaining pancakes.

**4**

Make the filling. Beat the cheese until smooth, then mix in the smoked salmon, spike with lemon juice to taste and season with pepper.

**5**

Divide the mixture between the centres of the pancakes. Top each with a little of the lumpfish roe. Carefully lift up the edges of the pancake to form a boat and secure with a cocktail stick (toothpick).

# Oriental Plum Chicken Wings *

Commercially prepared Chinese chicken just isn't a patch on these – and they are so simple to prepare!

**1**

Cut off and discard the wing tips from the chicken. Cut the wings into two pieces at the next joint.

**2**

Mix the remaining ingredients together in a large shallow baking tin (pan).

**3**

Add the chicken and turn to coat in the mixture. Leave to marinate for at least 1 hour.

**4**

Bake in a preheated oven at 180°C/350°F/gas mark 4 for about 1 hour, turning occasionally until tender and coated in a sticky glaze. Serve warm or cold.

| MAKES ABOUT 32 |
| --- |
| 900 g/2 lb chicken (buffalo) wings (not portions, just the wings) |
| 30 ml/2 tbsp wine vinegar |
| 60 ml/4 tbsp sunflower oil |
| 30 ml/2 tbsp soy sauce |
| 1 large garlic clove, crushed |
| 30 ml/2 tbsp golden (light corn) syrup |
| 30 ml/2 tbsp tomato purée (paste) |
| 30 ml/2 tbsp plum jam (conserve) |
| 15 ml/1 tbsp lemon juice |
| 5 ml/1 tsp ground ginger |

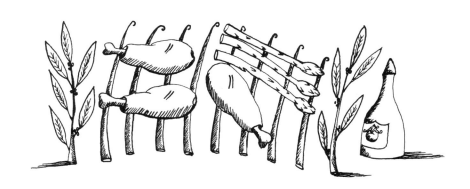

# Creamy Mushroom Whirls with Oregano*

These are so moreish they are irresistible – and so easy to make. They are best straight from the oven but can also be eaten cold.

### MAKES 24

6 slices of white bread, crusts removed

215 g/7½ oz/1 small can of creamed mushrooms

5 ml/1 tsp dried oregano

Salt and freshly ground black pepper

A little melted butter

30 ml/2 tbsp chopped parsley

A few sprigs of fresh oregano

**1**

Spread the bread with the creamed mushrooms and sprinkle with oregano. Season to taste with salt and pepper.

**2**

Roll up and cut each into four slices, securing the whirls with cocktail sticks (toothpicks).

**3**

Place on a baking (cookie) sheet, brush each with a little melted butter and sprinkle with parsley.

**4**

Bake in a preheated oven at 180°C/350°C/gas mark 4 for about 8–10 minutes until golden. Serve warm, garnished with fresh oregano.

# Cayenne-spiked Cheese Balls in Toasted Hazelnuts

The cheese and pineapple mixture is also good spread in celery sticks, cut into short lengths.

**1**

Mash the soft cheese with the drained pineapple, the Cheddar cheese and cayenne until well blended.

**2**

Shape into 30 small balls and roll in the toasted hazelnuts. Chill.

**3**

When ready to serve, spear each with half a pretzel stick, if liked.

| MAKES 30 |
| --- |
| 225 g/8 oz/1 cup medium-fat soft cheese |
| 90 ml/6 tbsp crushed pineapple, well drained |
| 175 g/6 oz/1½ cups strong Cheddar cheese, finely grated |
| 1.5 ml/¼ tsp cayenne |
| 100 g/4 oz/1 cup toasted chopped hazelnuts |
| Cocktail pretzel sticks (optional) |

# Melon and Parma Ham Morsels

Try substituting pieces of ripe pear for the melon for a more unusual combination.

**MAKES ABOUT 36**

1 small ripe melon

5 thin slices of Parma ham

18 cherry tomatoes, halved

**1**

Cut the melon into six wedges. Discard the seeds and cut off the skin. Then cut each wedge into six chunks.

**2**

Cut each slice of ham into six strips. Wrap a strip of ham around each piece of melon.

**3**

Place on cocktail sticks (toothpicks) with a halved cherry tomato on each.

# Chillied Crab Mangetout

These are a little fiddly to prepare but, once filled, they will keep perfectly fresh for several days if covered and placed in the fridge.

**1**

Plunge the mangetout into boiling water for 1 minute. Drain, rinse with cold water and drain again. Dry on kitchen paper (paper towels) and carefully make a slit in the side of each one to form a pocket.

**2**

Mash the remaining ingredients together and spoon into the mangetout. Chill until ready to serve.

### MAKES ABOUT 36

175 g/6 oz mangetout (snow peas)

200 g/7 oz/1 small can of crabmeat, drained

15 ml/1 tbsp mayonnaise

5 ml/1 tsp tomato purée (paste)

1 small green chilli, seeded and finely chopped

Salt and freshly ground black pepper

A few drops of lemon juice

# Crunchy Quark-stuffed Tomatoes

For an easy way to fill the tomatoes, put the quark mixture into a piping bag fitted with a large plain tube, then pipe it in.

### MAKES 24

24 cherry tomatoes

100 g/4 oz/½ cup quark

2 spring onions (scallions), finely chopped

1 celery stick, finely chopped

5 ml/1 tsp paprika

Salt and freshly ground black pepper

Poppy seeds

**1**

Cut a slice off the rounded end of the tomatoes and scoop out the seeds. Tip upside-down on kitchen paper (paper towels) to drain.

**2**

Mix the quark with the spring onions and celery and season with paprika, salt and pepper.

**3**

Spoon the mixture into the tomatoes and dust each with poppy seeds. Chill until ready to serve.

# Prawn Choux Balls ✳

Use any savoury mixture to fill choux balls – egg, ham, or chicken and mayonnaise; pâté mixed with soft cheese; or garlic and herb cheese. Freeze the unfilled choux balls.

## 1
Sift the flour and salt on to a sheet of greaseproof (waxed) paper. Place it next to the hob so it is ready to use later.

## 2
Heat the butter and water in a pan until the butter melts, then bring to the boil. Add the flour all in one go and beat with a wooden spoon until the mixture is smooth and leaves the sides of the pan clean. Remove from the heat.

## 3
Beat for 1 minute to cool, then gradually beat in the egg, beating well after each addition until the mixture is smooth and glossy but still holds its shape.

## 4
Spoon into 30 small balls on a greased baking (cookie) sheet and bake in a preheated oven at 220°C/425°F/ gas mark 7 for 7 minutes. Reduce the heat to 190°C/ 375°F/gas mark 5 and cook for a further 15 minutes until golden brown and crisp. Cool on a wire rack.

## 5
Mix the prawns with the mayonnaise and seasonings. Whip the cream until peaking and fold into the mixture with a metal spoon.

## 6
Make a small slit in the side of each choux ball and spoon the mixture inside.

| MAKES 30 |
| --- |
| PASTRY (PASTE): |
| 65 g/2½ oz/scant ¾ cup plain (all-purpose) flour |
| Pinch of salt |
| 25 g/1 oz/2 tbsp butter |
| 150 ml/¼ pt/⅔ cup water |
| 1 egg, beaten |
| FILLING: |
| 100 g/4 oz peeled prawns (shrimp), roughly chopped |
| 60 ml/4 tbsp mayonnaise |
| Pinch of cayenne |
| 5 ml/1 tsp anchovy essence (extract) |
| Freshly ground black pepper |
| 150 ml/¼ pt/⅔ cup double (heavy) cream |

# Olive and Prune Turkey Fries ❄

These are a colourful and very elegant variation on Scotch eggs.

| MAKES 30 |
| --- |
| 450 g/1 lb turkey sausages |
| 15 stuffed green olives |
| 15 ready-to-eat prunes, stoned (pitted) |
| 50 g/2 oz/1 cup fresh breadcrumbs |
| 15 ml/1 tsp paprika |
| 1 egg, beaten |
| Oil for deep-frying |

**1**

Skin the sausages and knead the meat into one large sausage shape. Cut into 15 equal pieces. Flatten each piece.

**2**

Push an olive into the stone cavity of each prune.

**3**

Put a stuffed prune in the centre of each piece of sausagemeat and wrap the sausagemeat around.

**4**

Mix the breadcrumbs with the paprika. Roll the sausage balls in beaten egg, then the breadcrumb mix to coat completely.

**5**

Deep-fry in hot oil for 8 minutes until cooked through and golden brown. Drain on kitchen paper. Leave to cool.

**6**

Cut into halves to serve.

# Caramelised Onion and Camembert Filo Bites

For maximum flavour, cook the onions very slowly but really thoroughly until rich and brown. Don't let them burn, though!

### 1

Melt two-thirds of the butter in a large frying pan (skillet). Add the onions and fry (sauté) for 3 minutes, stirring until softened. Sprinkle the sugar over and continue to cook, stirring, until a rich golden brown (about 5 minutes). Season well with salt and pepper.

### 2

Melt the remaining butter. Lay a sheet of pastry on a board and cut into thirds widthways. Brush each sheet with a little of the butter and fold in half widthways. Brush again.

### 3

Divide the onion mixture into 24 and spoon a portion in the centre of each piece of pastry. Sprinkle with a little of the basil. Top with a wedge of Camembert and fold the pastry over to form neat parcels.

### 4

Transfer to a buttered baking sheet, folded sides down. Brush with melted butter.

### 5

Repeat with the remaining sheets of pastry and filling.

### 6

Bake in a preheated oven at 190°C/375°F/gas mark 5 for about 10 minutes until golden. Serve warm.

| MAKES 24 |
| --- |
| 75 g/3 oz/⅓ cup butter |
| 2 Spanish onions, halved and thinly sliced |
| 30 ml/2 tbsp caster (superfine) sugar |
| Salt and freshly ground black pepper |
| 8 large sheets of filo pastry (paste) |
| 45 ml/3 tbsp chopped basil |
| 2 Camembert rounds, each cut into 12 wedges |

# Gruyère and Fennel Seed Straws

Caraway seeds are a delicious alternative to fennel seeds. For a more delicate flavour, use Cheddar cheese and sesame seeds.

### MAKES ABOUT 48

100 g/4 oz/1 cup plain (all-purpose) flour

Pinch of salt

Freshly ground black pepper

50 g/2 oz/¼ cup butter

75 g/3 oz/¾ cup Gruyère (Swiss) cheese, finely grated

1 egg, separated

A little water

45 ml/3 tbsp fennel seeds

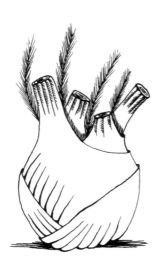

**1**

Sift the flour into a bowl. Add the salt and a good grinding of pepper. Rub in the butter and stir in the Gruyère. Mix with the egg yolk, adding a little water if necessary, to form a firm dough.

**2**

Knead gently on a lightly floured surface and roll out to a rectangle about 5 mm/¼ thick. Trim the edges, then brush with the egg white and sprinkle with the fennel seeds.

**3**

Cut the dough into strips about 7.5 cm/3 in wide, then cut each strip into short strips about the width of a little finger.

**4**

Roll out the trimmings into thin strings and make a plait. Cut it into eight pieces and shape into rounds. Lay the straws and plaited rounds on a lightly greased baking sheet.

**5**

Bake in a preheated oven at 180°C/350°F/gas mark 4 for about 7 minutes until golden. Cool on a wire rack and store in an airtight tin. To serve, place six straws in each of the plaited rings.

# Cunning Quick Canapés

Large platters, offering a selection of these simple canapés, look very impressive but take very little time to prepare.

- Tiny bite-sized smoked salmon sandwiches.

- Canned asparagus spears, drained and placed individually on thin slices of buttered bread (crusts removed), rolled up and cut into pinwheels.

- Cocktail sausages on sticks (toothpicks) with bought salsa (or use the recipe on page 81) dip.

- Small round crackers topped with: liver pâté, smoked salmon or smoked mackerel pâté and a tiny piece of lemon; sliced hard-boiled (hard-cooked) egg and a tiny portion of Danish lumpfish roe; salami and a slice of olive; thinly sliced ham with a tiny piece of tomato; cream cheese and a walnut half.

- Oven-baked scampi in breadcrumbs on sticks with tartare sauce to dip.

- Mini Chicken Kievs on sticks.

- Cocktail pitta breads filled with: taramasalata; hummus; chopped egg mayonnaise; chopped cooked prawns (shrimp) in cocktail sauce; flavoured cottage cheese.

# White Chocolate Mini Florentines

For an even more stunning effect, cover half the florentines in white chocolate and half in dark chocolate.

| MAKES ABOUT 36 |
| --- |
| 100 g/4 oz/½ cup butter |
| 150 g/5 oz/⅔ cup caster (superfine) sugar |
| 25 g/1 oz/¼ cup glacé (candied) cherries, finely chopped |
| 100 g/4 oz/1 cup chopped almonds |
| 40 g/1½ oz/⅓ cup flaked (slivered) almonds |
| 100 g/4 oz/1 cup chopped mixed (candied) peel |
| 30 ml/2 tbsp double (heavy) cream, whipped |
| 100 g/4 oz white chocolate |

**1**

Line two baking (cookie) sheets with non-stick baking parchment as the mixture tends to be a bit sticky.

**2**

Melt the butter and sugar in a pan and bring to the boil. Remove from the heat. Add the cherries, nuts and peel. Stir in the whipped cream and cool until stiff.

**3**

Put 2.5 ml/½ tsp mounds of the mixture well apart on the baking sheets. Bake in a preheated oven at 180°C/350°F/gas mark 4 for about 6 minutes until golden and bubbling. Leave to cool.

**4**

Melt the chocolate in a bowl over a pan of hot water (or in the microwave). Loosen the biscuits (cookies) from the baking sheets and spread the undersides with a little of the chocolate. Leave chocolate-sides up on a wire rack to set. Store in an airtight container.

# Rum and Almond Truffles *

These are delicious served with coffee after a dinner party too.

| MAKES 24 |
| --- |
| 60 ml/4 tbsp plain (semi-sweet) chocolate spread |
| 75 g/3 oz/¾ cup cake crumbs |
| 25 g/1 oz/¼ cup ground almonds |
| Rum |
| Cocoa (unsweetened chocolate) powder |

**1**

Mix the chocolate spread with the cake crumbs and almonds, stirring until the ingredients are well blended.

**2**

Add enough rum to form a soft but not sticky dough.

**3**

Roll the mixture into 24 small balls, then roll in cocoa powder to coat.

**4**

Place in petit four paper cases (candy cups) and chill.

# Ginger Cream Baskets

You will need two table-tennis balls for this recipe! The snaps are a little time-consuming, but not difficult, to prepare, but the results are well worth it!

| MAKES 16 |
| --- |
| 25 g/1 oz/2 tbsp butter |
| 25 g/1 oz/2 tbsp caster (superfine) sugar |
| 15 ml/1 tbsp golden (light corn) syrup |
| 25 g/1 oz/¼ cup plain (all-purpose) flour |
| 1.5 ml/¼ tsp ground ginger |
| 2.5 ml/½ tsp brandy |
| A little oil |
| FILLING: |
| 150 ml/¼ pt/⅔ cup double (heavy) cream |
| 30 ml/2 tbsp ginger syrup from a jar of stem ginger |
| 2 pieces of stem ginger, finely chopped |
| A little extra ground ginger |

**1**

Line a baking (cookie) sheet with non-stick baking parchment as the mixture tends to be sticky.

**2**

Melt the butter, sugar and syrup in a saucepan. Stir in the flour, ginger and brandy.

**3**

Drop 2.5 ml/½ tsp mounds of the mixture well apart on the baking sheet.

**4**

Bake in a preheated oven at 180°C/350°F/gas mark 4 for 7–10 minutes or until the outer ones are golden and bubbly.

**5**

Meanwhile, brush two table-tennis balls with oil.

**6**

Remove the baking sheet from the oven and quickly mould two of the brownest snaps round the balls. Twist out the balls as soon as the snaps are set and repeat with two more. Return to the oven in between to continue to cook the remaining snaps. When cold, store in an airtight container until ready to fill.

**7**

Whip the cream until peaking and whisk in the ginger syrup. Fold in the chopped ginger. Chill. Spoon the ginger into the cases and dust with ground ginger.

# Raspberry Hazelnut Meringues

These bite-sized meringues can be served unfilled as an accompaniment to fresh fruit salads for a dessert.

### 1
*L*ine a baking (cookie) sheet with non-stick baking parchment as the mixture tends to be sticky.

### 2
Whisk the egg whites until stiff. Whisk in half the sugar and continue whisking until glossy. Fold in the remaining sugar, the vanilla essence and the nuts.

### 3
Using two teaspoons, shape the meringue into 24 small oval mounds on the baking sheet.

### 4
Bake in a preheated oven at 120°C/250°F/gas mark ½ for about 2 hours until dried out. Cool on a wire rack. Store in an airtight tin until ready to fill.

### 5
Mash the raspberries. Whip the cream until stiff. Fold the fruit into the cream and sweeten to taste with sifted icing sugar. Chill until ready to use.

### 6
Sandwich the meringues together in pairs with a little of the cream filling.

| MAKES 12 |
| --- |
| 2 egg whites |
| 100 g/4 oz/½ cup caster (superfine) sugar |
| 5 ml/1 tsp vanilla essence (extract) |
| 50 g/2 oz/½ cup ground hazelnuts |
| FILLING: |
| 75 g/3 oz raspberries |
| 150 ml/¼ pt/⅔ cup double (heavy) cream |
| Icing (confectioners') sugar, to taste |

# Apricot Cinnamon Croûtes

Any sort of plums can be substituted for the apricots but make sure they are canned in juice – syrup would make the croûtes just too sweet.

### MAKES ABOUT 24

2 × 410 g/14½ oz/large cans apricot halves in natural juice, drained

6–8 thick slices of bread from a large sliced loaf

Butter, softened

90 ml/6 tbsp caster (superfine) sugar

15 ml/1 tbsp ground cinnamon

150 ml/¼ pt/⅔ cup crème fraîche

1

Count the number of apricots. Cut out the same number of rounds from the bread, using a 5 cm/2 in cutter.

2

Butter the bread on both sides, then fry (sauté) in a frying pan (skillet) until golden brown on both sides.

3

Mix the sugar and cinnamon together and toss the fried bread round in it to coat completely. (Use a little more sugar, if necessary.)

4

Put a spoonful of crème fraîche on each croûte and top with an apricot half, rounded side up.

# Summer Fruit Tartlets

You can cheat and buy tiny ready-made pastry cases (shells), making these deliciously fresh little tarts so simple to prepare.

**1**

Sift the flour into a bowl. Add the butter and rub in with the fingertips until the mixture resembles breadcrumbs. Stir in the sugar.

**2**

Beat the egg yolk and water together and stir into the mixture to form a firm dough.

**3**

Knead gently on a lightly floured surface, then wrap and chill for at least 30 minutes.

**4**

Roll out and use to line 4 cm/1½ in petit four tartlet tins (pans). Place a piece of crumpled foil in each case (shell) and bake in a preheated oven at 200°C/400°F/ gas mark 6 for 8 minutes. Remove the foil, brush the insides with the egg white and bake for a further 5 minutes until golden brown. Transfer to a wire rack to cool.

**5**

Meanwhile, put the fruits, sugar and liqueur in a saucepan. Heat gently until the sugar melts and the juices begin to run but the fruits are still whole. Leave to cool.

**6**

When ready to serve, put 2.5 ml/½ tsp lemon curd in the base of each tartlet. Spoon in the gently stewed fruits with a tiny drop of their juices. Top each with a piece of strawberry and serve.

| MAKES 16 | | |
| --- | --- | --- |
| **SWEET PASTRY (PASTE):** | | |
| 150 g/5 oz/1¼ cups plain (all-purpose) flour | | |
| 75 g/3 oz/⅓ cup butter, cut into small pieces | | |
| 10 ml/2 tsp caster (superfine) sugar | | |
| 1 egg, separated | | |
| 10 ml/2 tsp water | | |
| **FILLING:** | | |
| 350 g/12 oz mixed soft fruits (redcurrants, blackcurrants, whitecurrants, raspberries) | | |
| 50 g/2 oz/¼ cup caster (superfine) sugar | | |
| 30 ml/2 tbsp orange liqueur | | |
| 40 ml/8 tsp lemon curd | | |
| 4 small strawberries, quartered lengthways | | |

# Brandy-chocolate Choux Buns \*

Baby profiteroles are irresistible. Try flavouring the cream with mashed fresh strawberries instead of chocolate.

| MAKES 30 |
| --- |
| 1 quantity of choux pastry (paste) (see Prawn Choux Balls, page 147) |
| FILLING: |
| 300 ml/½ pt/1¼ cups double (heavy) cream, whipped |
| 175 g/6 oz plain (semi-sweet) chocolate |
| 30 ml/2 tbsp brandy |
| TO DECORATE: |
| Icing (confectioners') sugar, sifted |

1
Make the choux balls according to the recipe, baking them until golden and then leaving them to cool.

2
Make the filling. Whip the cream. Melt the chocolate in a bowl over a pan of hot water or in the microwave. Stir in the brandy, then fold into the cream. Use to fill the choux balls.

3
Pile on a serving plate and dust with icing sugar.

# Dolcellatte, Camembert and Grape Kebabs

Though not sweet, these are a tasty way to round off a meal, especially for those who have no room for a proper dessert! You can use stoned (pitted) olives instead of grapes.

| MAKES 16 |
| --- |
| 32 green seedless (pitless) grapes |
| 100 g/4 oz Red Leicester cheese |
| 32 black seedless (pitless) grapes |
| 100 g/4 oz Dolcelatte |
| 100 g/4 oz Camembert or Brie |
| TO SERVE: |
| Lettuce leaves |

1
Cut each of the cheeses into 16 cubes and thread with the grapes on cocktail sticks (toothpicks), arranging attractively, to make 16 little kebabs.

2
Serve on a bed of fresh lettuce leaves.

# Cherry and Kirsch Strudels ✳

Make baby apple strudels in the same way: simply substitute peeled and chopped cooking (tart) apple for the cherries and add 2.5 ml/½ tsp cinnamon instead of the kirsch.

### 1
Lay the pastry sheets on a work surface and brush with melted butter. Cut each piece into quarters, fold each quarter in half again and brush with a little more butter.

### 2
Mix the almonds and sugar together and sprinkle over the surface of the 16 pieces of pastry.

### 3
Scatter the cherries over and drizzle a few drops of kirsch over each, if liked.

### 4
Fold in the edges of two opposite sides of the pastry and roll up each to form a small sausage shape.

### 5
Transfer to a buttered baking sheet and brush with a little more melted butter.

### 6
Bake in a preheated oven at 190°C/375°F/gas mark 5 for about 10 minutes or until golden brown. Cool on a wire rack. Dust with a little sifted icing sugar before serving.

| MAKES 16 |
| --- |
| 4 sheets of filo pastry (paste) |
| 30 ml/2 tbsp melted butter |
| FILLING: |
| 60 ml/4 tbsp ground almonds |
| 60 ml/4 tbsp caster (superfine) sugar |
| 225 g/8 oz cherries, stoned (pitted) and roughly chopped |
| 30 ml/2 tbsp kirsch (optional) |
| TO DECORATE: |
| A little sifted icing (confectioners') sugar |

# Coffee and Walnut Butterflies ✳

Make chocolate cakes, if you prefer, by substituting cocoa (unsweetened chocolate) powder for the coffee.

### MAKES 24

CAKES:

50 g/2 oz/¼ cup soft tub margarine

50 g/2 oz/¼ cup caster (superfine) sugar

1 egg

50 g/2 oz/½ cup self-raising (self-rising) flour

2.5 ml/½ tsp baking powder

20 ml/4 tsp instant coffee powder

10 ml/2 tsp water

50 g/2 oz/½ cup walnuts, finely chopped

FILLING:

100 g/4 oz/½ cup cream cheese

10 ml/2 tsp brandy

15 ml/1 tbsp icing (confectioners') sugar

**1**

Put the margarine, sugar, egg, flour and baking powder in a mixing bowl. Beat together until smooth and light.

**2**

Dissolve half of the coffee in the water and beat into the mixture with the walnuts.

**3**

Use to fill 24 petit four paper cases (candy cups) on a baking sheet.

**4**

Bake in a preheated oven at 180°C/350°F/gas mark 4 for about 8 minutes until risen and golden and the centres spring back when lightly pressed. Cool on a wire rack.

**5**

Put the cheese in a bowl. Blend the remaining coffee with the brandy and sugar. Beat into the cheese.

**6**

Cut a round out of the top of each cake, making a shallow hollow with a rim of cake. Spoon in the coffee cheese filling.

**7**

Cut the rounds of cake in half to make two semi-circles and press at an angle in the top of each cake to represent butterfly wings.

# Campfire Magic

If you are camping in a tent or caravan you are likely to have only the minimum of cooking facilities – perhaps two gas rings at most. And if you are a really seasoned camper, you'll be slaving over a smoking wood fire in the back of beyond. Either way, good tucker is a must. Here are just a few simple but sumptuous meals, using the most basic of equipment and utensils. They can all be cooked on a gas ring or on an open fire.

## KNOW-HOW

Make sure you take with you:

- Matches and tapers.

- Firelighters (if you are making a real fire), in case the wood is damp.

- A large saucepan with a lid.

- A large frying pan (skillet), preferably with a lid.

- A grill (broiler) rack.

- Your favourite cook's knife.

- A wooden spoon and fish slice.

- Kitchen paper (paper towels).

- Heavy-duty foil.

- Oven gloves.

- Can opener.

- For drinks, see Family Picnics, page 9, for useful ideas.

# One-pot Meals

# Char-grilled Pepperoni Pizza

Take a flask of hot water to make the dough, or heat cold water on the fire before you start to make the pizza.

**1**

Cover a grill (broiler) rack with heavy-duty foil, or two thicknesses of ordinary foil, and then oil the foil.

**2**

Mix the pizza dough with water according to the packet directions. Knead in the bowl, then flatten between your hands to make a large, fairly thin round.

**3**

Place the dough round on the foil and cook over the fire (or lay the grill rack over the gas flames) for about 6–8 minutes until browned underneath. (You'll need to rotate the rack several times if cooking over gas flames to ensure more even cooking.) Turn over and spread the cooked side with tomato purée. Sprinkle with oregano, then top with pepperoni and the cheese.

**4**

Cover loosely with foil and continue cooking for a further 10 minutes or until the cheese has melted and the pizza is cooked through. (Again, you'll need to rotate the rack if over gas flames.) Serve straight away, cut into wedges or quarters.

| SERVES 4 |
|---|
| Oil |
| 280 g/10 oz/1 packet pizza base mix |
| Hand-hot water |
| 50 g/2 oz/½ tube tomato purée (paste) |
| Dried oregano |
| 50 g/2 oz pepperoni or chorizo sausage, sliced |
| 100 g/4 oz/1 cup Mozzarella cheese, grated |

# Okra and Prawn Pilau

Toss in any other favourite vegetables – mushrooms are particularly good in this dish.

| SERVES 4 |
| --- |
| 1 onion, chopped |
| 4 rashers (slices) of streaky bacon, rinded and diced |
| 15 ml/1 tbsp sunflower or olive oil |
| 225 g/8 oz okra, cut into chunky slices |
| 225 g/8 oz/1 cup long-grain rice |
| 5 ml/1 tsp ground cumin |
| 600 ml/1 pt/2½ cups water |
| 1 chicken stock cube |
| Salt and freshly ground black pepper |
| 225 g/8 oz peeled prawns (shrimp) |
| Chopped parsley (optional) |

1
In a large pan, fry (sauté) the onion and bacon in the oil until just softening, stirring the mixture all the time.

2
Stir in the okra, rice and cumin and cook for about 1 minute until well coated in the oil.

3
Add the remaining ingredients except the prawns and parsley, cover and simmer for about 15 minutes. Add the prawns, cover and cook for a further 5 minutes or until the rice is tender and has absorbed the liquid. Taste and re-season, if necessary.

4
Sprinkle with chopped parsley, if using, and serve straight from the pot.

# Sausage and Passata Skillet

Sausage is the perfect meat for a lazy cook, needing no effort but providing lots of taste. Wash this down with very cold lager.

**1**

Fry (sauté) the sausages in the oil in a large frying pan (skillet) for 2 minutes, stirring until the fat starts to run.

**2**

Add the potatoes, herbs, onion granules (if using) and a little salt and pepper and fry, stirring, until the potatoes and sausages are golden.

**3**

Add the mushrooms and sweetcorn and continue cooking for 5 minutes, stirring.

**4**

Drizzle the passata over the top, cover with a lid and cook for 2 minutes until piping hot.

**5**

Serve straight from the pan with crusty bread.

| SERVES 4 |
|---|
| 8 chipolata sausages, cut into chunks |
| 15 ml/1 tbsp sunflower or olive oil |
| 425 g/15 oz/1 large can of potatoes, drained |
| 2.5 ml/½ tsp dried mixed herbs |
| 5 ml/1 tsp onion granules (optional) |
| Salt and freshly ground black pepper |
| 298 g/10½ oz/1 small can of button mushrooms, drained |
| 200 g/7 oz/1 small can of sweetcorn (corn), drained |
| 300 ml/½ pt/1¼ cups passata (sieved tomatoes) |
| TO SERVE: |
| Crusty bread |

# Speedy Garlic Pasta with Salami

If you use ham, a good pinch of dried mint will really complement the flavour.

| SERVES 4 |
| --- |
| 225 g/8 oz pasta shapes |
| 100 g/4 oz salami or ham, chopped |
| 1 garlic clove, chopped, or a squeeze from a tube of garlic purée (paste) |
| 298 g/10½ oz/1 small can of garden peas, drained |
| 2 eggs |
| 60 ml/4 tbsp milk |
| Salt and freshly ground black pepper |
| Parmesan cheese, grated |

**1**

Put a large pan of water on to boil. When bubbling, add the pasta and cook for about 10 minutes until just tender. Drain and return the pasta to the pan.

**2**

Add the salami or ham, garlic and peas and heat through for 2 minutes, stirring.

**3**

Beat the eggs and milk together with a little salt and pepper and stir into the pot. Cook, stirring, until creamy but don't scramble the eggs completely.

**4**

Spoon on to plates and sprinkle with grated Parmesan cheese.

# Swiss-style Pork with Caraway

If you do not want to use the whole cabbage, any left-over raw cabbage can be mixed with grated carrot and mayonnaise, to make coleslaw.

**1**

Cook the sliced potatoes in boiling, lightly salted water until just tender. Drain, reserving the cooking water, and put to one side.

**2**

In the same pan, fry (sauté) the pork in the oil until browned on both sides. Remove from the pan.

**3**

Add the cabbage and caraway to the pan and toss in the oil to coat completely. Cook for a few minutes until it begins to soften.

**4**

Press down and lay the pork on top. Season well.

**5**

Cover with a layer of the cooked potatoes.

**6**

Crumble the stock cube into 300 ml/½ pt/1¼ cups of the reserved potato water. Pour into the pan. Cover and cook for about 30 minutes until the meat is cooked through. Divide between four serving plates and serve.

| SERVES 4 |
| --- |
| 3 large potatoes, sliced |
| 4 pork chops or steaks |
| 15 ml/1 tbsp sunflower or olive oil |
| 1 small white cabbage, finely shredded |
| 15 ml/1 tbsp caraway seeds |
| Salt and freshly ground black pepper |
| 1 chicken stock cube |

# Mexican Tacos

This chilli mixture can also be used to fill flour tortillas, if you prefer, with the same accompaniments.

| SERVES 4 |
|---|
| 350 g/12 oz minced (ground) beef or lamb |
| 2.5 ml/½ tsp chilli powder (or to taste) |
| 5 ml/1 tsp ground cumin |
| 5 ml/1 tsp dried oregano |
| 1 garlic clove, crushed, or a squeeze from a tube of garlic purée (paste) |
| 400 g/14 oz/1 large can of chopped tomatoes |
| 425 g/15 oz/1 large can of red kidney beans, drained |
| 15 ml/1 tbsp tomato purée |
| TO SERVE: |
| 12 taco shells |
| Shredded lettuce |
| Grated cheese |
| Chilli salsa or tomato relish |
| Soured (dairy sour) cream (optional) |

1

Fry (sauté) the meat in a saucepan until well browned, stirring constantly to make sure all the grains are separate.

2

Add the remaining ingredients. Cover and cook for about 30 minutes until the mixture is rich and thick, stirring from time to time.

3

To serve, spoon the mixture into the taco shells, top with a little shredded lettuce, grated cheese, chilli salsa or tomato relish and soured cream, if liked, and eat with the fingers.

# Index